Stop I

CW01511803

How to Stop Dieting and Eat Normally

The Best Healthy Weight Loss
Foods to Eat

3rd Edition

By Nicholas Bjorn

Nicholas Bjorn

Nicholas Bjorn

Table of Contents

Introduction

This book includes proven steps and strategies on how you can boost energy and burn fat, plus the best fat burning super foods you should be eating for healthy weight loss.

If you have tried to lose weight before, you know it's not always easy. With so many diets to choose from and each telling you're a different way to eat and what foods to avoid; it can easily get confusing or frustrating. That's why this book focuses on normal foods you can actually eat to not only lose weight, but also improve your health.

If you are truly serious about losing weight and are prepared to make the commitment to eating healthier, then this is the book for you.

Nicholas Bjorn

FREE E-BOOKS SENT WEEKLY

Join <u>North Star Readers Book Club</u>
And Get Exclusive Access To The Latest Kindle Books in
Health, Fitness, Weight Loss and Much More…

TO GET YOU STARTED HERE IS YOUR FREE E-BOOK:

Visit to Sign Up Today!
<u>www.northstarreaders.com/weight-loss-kick-start</u>

Nicholas Bjorn

Chapter 1 – 10 Nutrition Rules for Boosting Energy Burning Fat

Everyone wants to feel good, to feel alert, rested and full of energy but, for most, this is just a dream. The reality is we live in a harsh world, where time is in short supply and stress is in abundance. Lack of sleep combined with poor diet and stress leads to illness and exhaustion.

Fatigue is one of the worst things for the human body; it breaks us down emotionally and physically and it wreaks total havoc on our immune systems, which opens the way for chronic disease. But we all have the power needed to make that change, to give our bodies the energy boost they need and to feel fantastic with it.

Regular exercise, learning how to manage stress and sleeping properly are all critical factors in being able to combat fatigue but you can also make a change to your eating habits. The following are ten ways in which you can use the food you eat to give you energy that lasts throughout the day.

Rule Number 1 – Eat Foods that are Dense in Nutrients

The best way to boost your metabolism to convert your food into energy is eat foods that contain the right minerals and vitamins – and plenty of them. If you eat the right food, all the cells in your body will produce energy to keep you going.

Rule Number 2 – Eat Foods that are High in Antioxidants

These are the scavengers that clean out all the chemicals and toxins in the body that are wearing you down. Eat plenty of fruits and vegetables and other plant-based foods rather than taking them in supplement form. Eating too much of some nutrients can be risky so get round this by eating only whole foods, like colorful berries, melons and dark green leafy vegetables.

Rule Number 3 – Eating your Omega-3's

Over the years, research has shown that plenty of omega-3 in your diet can improve your memory, mood and thinking, all of which are closely related to energy. Try to eat one good helping per day in the form of flax oil or seeds, fish, hemp oil or seeds, leafy greens and walnuts.

Rule Number 4 – Stop Dieting

Most diets are no good for the human body because they require you to deprive your body of certain foods. You should not cut your calories down too much because this just decreases your metabolism. That is why many people who are on strict diets often complain of lethargy. And, as your metabolism slows down, your body will burn off less calories, which means the ultimate result, is a gain in weight. Eat the right amount of calorie needs every day and eat them in the right foods, combined with regular exercise if you want to successfully drop the pounds.

Rule Number 5 – Don't Skip Breakfast

Yes, it is so easy, when you are running late and there are those who think that to lose weight they have to skip a meal. It is the wrong meal to skip. Breakfast is the most important meal of the day as it gets your metabolism off and running and a good breakfast will keep your energy levels up until it's time for lunch. Instead of hitting the bagel bar or eating stodgy cereals, go for eggs, fresh fruit, whole grain cereal and nuts.

Rule Number 6 – Don't Pass on Snacks

It is important to eat enough of the right foods to keep you blood glucose levels steady throughout the day, and that will keep your energy levels steady as well. Snack on dried fruit and nuts, yoghurt with granola, whole grain crackers, fresh raw vegetables and fruits.

Rule Number 7 – Drink Your Fluids

Hydration is an important part of weight loss and of keeping your energy levels high. Your body needs a lot of water to function at its best but, unless you are doing endurance training, skip the energy drinks and vitamin waters. Instead, drink plain water or water with fresh fruit chunks in it and aim to drink at least one cup every couple of hours.

Rule Number 8 – Be a Designated Driver

That will help you to cut out one of the biggest enemies of those who want to lose weight – alcohol. As well as acting as a depressant, alcohol can also act as a stimulant, interrupting your sleep patterns and causing tiredness the following day. If you are relying on a drink every night to help you fall asleep, you are doing the wrong thing. Cutting out the alcohol will help you to sleep better.

If you do want to have a drink occasionally, stick to red wine. It is an antioxidant but do be aware that you cannot drink if you are on certain medications, have high blood pressure or anxiety.

Rule Number 9 – Caffeine – Little or None

Caffeine should be used carefully and in small amounts. Although it seems as if it is giving you an energy boost, it won't last for long and you will know it when it wears off. And never use caffeine as a meal replacement! Green tea is a better choice of caffeine as it also contains antioxidants and theanine, which is an essential amino acid that helps you to stay calm.

Rule Number 10 – Eat Power Foods

Try to stick to nutritional foods that provide energy, a list of 10 are below. Later on I will go into more details on foods to eat to help you burn off fat.

- Nuts, especially almonds

- Avocado

- Dark leafy greens, such as watercress, kale, spinach, collard or beet greens

- Whole grains that are intact, like quinoa, millet, brown rice or amaranth

- Ground flax seeds

- White beans, lentils, black beans

- Dried fruits such as dates but in moderation

- Berries – blackberries, strawberries, raspberries, blueberries, etc.

- Sea vegetables such as Nori, hijiki, dulse, etc.

- Edamame – whole young soy beans

Nicholas Bjorn

Chapter 2 – Top 10 Herbs and Spices to Help Improve Health and Weight Loss

Herbs and spices are a fantastic way of giving otherwise bland food a taste boost and using them is one of the best ways to enjoy nutritious foods that may not taste so great. Not many people know that herbs and spices are full of health benefits. The following are ten of the best to boost your health and excite your taste buds.

Cayenne Pepper

Adds a dash of spice and also helps to enhance bodily functions. Cayenne helps to boost the metabolism, in turn increasing the amount of fat that your body burns off and it improves your blood flow. This means that the essential nutrients and vitamins in your food are moved through the body far more efficiently, allowing your body to function better.

Black Pepper

Similar to cayenne, black pepper helps to boost the metabolism and it helps to improve the digestive process, which in turn helps the body to shed weight. It also contains anti-cancer properties.

Nicholas Bjorn

Ginger

Ginger is good for suppressing the appetite and aiding digestion. It also works to warm up the body, increasing metabolism and helping more calories to burn off. Ginger is good for shifting toxins out of the body, in particular out of the fat cells.

Ginseng

Ginseng helps to boost metabolism and raise energy levels and is popular in energy drinks. It is a great one to use just before you do short high intensity workouts.

Chamomile Tea

Chamomile tea is great for relaxation and helps to reduce stress levels. It also helps to stop emotional eating in the evenings, thus preventing weight gain and it helps you to sleep better. Chamomile contains anti-inflammatory properties, helping to reduce the inflammation that causes so many different diseases, and it is high in antioxidants, eliminating free radicals from the body.

Cumin

Cumin tends to be mixed with other spices to give a nice flavor to Mexican, Indian, Middle Eastern and Mediterranean foods. It is used as a part of Ayurvedic medicine, helps to boost your immune system, decrease your cholesterol and contains anti-oxidant properties. It helps to increase the energy levels, allowing for more calories to be burned off.

Turmeric

Turmeric is fantastic for people who crave junk food. It helps to boost the function of the liver and to balance out hormones, which also prevents binges. It is a powerful antioxidant that helps to maintain good joints and skin, as well as vision. It works to enhance the immune system, digestive processes and the function of the liver as well as stabilizing blood glucose levels and cutting down on the amount of fat storage.

Cinnamon

This is a sweet spice that helps to boost metabolism and improve insulin sensitivity, thus helping to boost fat burning and control the blood sugar levels.

Mustard

Mustard helps to boost weight loss because it is full of B-complex vitamins, such as niacin, folates, riboflavin and thiamine, all of which increase the metabolism. One teaspoon of mustard can help to boost metabolism by 25%. Mustard is also high in magnesium and selenium which provides anti-inflammatory properties to help fight off disease. It is also a good source of zeaxanthins, carotenes and luteins, all of which are good antioxidants that help to eliminate free radicals.

Cardamom

This is a sweet spice that is used in Indian cooking and it helps to promote a healthy digestion and increases your metabolism. It is a commonly used ingredient in Ayurvedic medicine and has been shown to help mouth ulcers, high blood pressure, and depression. It has both anti-oxidative and anti-inflammatory properties and can also help to slow down the aging process.

So, the next time you are preparing your meals, add in one or more of these herbs and spices. Not only will your food taste nicer, your health will be better and your metabolism will be faster, helping you to burn off fat more efficiently.

Chapter 3 – 36 Fat Burning Super Foods

Food is not our enemy but so many diets will have you believe that it is. You don't need to eat a diet that is lacking in taste or looks to lose weight and you certainly do not need to deprive yourself just because the latest fad diet says you mustn't at certain foods. The following 36 foods are super foods that will help you to burn off fat more efficiently. However, don't get stuck on just one of them; introduce a few of them at a time to your weekly menu and, as time goes on, you will find that you are eating more and more of them.

Tomatoes

Who really cares if a tomato is a fruit or a vegetable? All that is important is knowing that a tomato contains loads of goodness that can help your body in the long terms and, over the short term, it can help you to lose some weight. They are low in calories but contain enough fiber to keep you regular and make you feel fuller. Tomatoes contain lycopene as well, which are antioxidants, helpful in removing free radicals and other toxins from your system.

Oranges

Oranges are full of vitamin C, which is needed to keep your body functioning at an optimal level. However, many people avoid oranges when they are trying to burn fat because they are worried about the sugar level. Oranges do contain sugar and, if you eat too many of them and don't burn off the sugar, it can turn to fat. However, they are low in calories and high in fiber, which helps keep your glucose levels regular. To help you to lose weight, moderate how much you eat and use it as a way of curbing a craving for candy.

Oats

Oats contain fiber, which helps to boost the metabolism, although many of those who do diets like Atkins and Paleo would disagree. A bowl of oatmeal is a fabulous way to start off the day. It isn't just full of fiber; it also contains anti-oxidants and lots of other minerals. Oats are a good way of cutting cholesterol levels.

Spices

You do not need to eat bland tasteless food when you are trying to shed some pounds so get experimenting with the contents of your spice rack. Some of them contain thermo genic properties, which help to boost the metabolism, and all of them give dishes a great taste. Mustard seed goes great on an entrée and will boost your metabolism while ginger helps your digestive system. Ginseng boosts energy and black pepper can help you to burn off calories. Turmeric is good for breaking up fat.

Sweet Potatoes

These are a fantastic addition to a diet, as a replacement for normal potatoes because they contain fewer calories and can help you to feel fuller for longer. Sweet potatoes are also loaded with potassium, fiber, vitamin B6 and vitamin C, making them the perfect replacement for a food that is normally shunned by dieters everywhere.

Apples

Not many people realize just how good an apple is. They are sweet enough to be a good replacement for sweet cravings and you can easily see why they end up in desserts. They are also low in calories, low in fat and low in sodium while being high in fiber. The fiber fills you up for longer and stops you from eating in between meals, and they also help with your digestive system too. Make sure you chew and apple thoroughly to get the best out of it.

Nuts

Every diet plan in the world include nuts and they are the one food that unites the vegetarians with the meat loving paleo dieters. They come straight from the earth and a small handful of nuts, raw and organic ones like pecans, walnuts or almonds, can be a tasty and filling snack that keep soya going for a few hours. You can also chop them and add them to a salad or sprinkle them over your food. Nuts are full of good healthy fats and full of flavor.

Quinoa

Quinoa is just starting to become popular in mainstream diets and the weight loss normally happens when you switch out rice or potatoes, or other starchy sides with quinoa. You get the full benefits of a well-rounded meals with all the vitamins contained in the quinoa. It is low in calories, low GI and full of taste.

Beans

Beans are a staple part of many diets and should be included as part of your weekly menu. They help to regulate glucose levels, help with digestion because of their high fiber content and are a great replacement for high carb foods. Black beans are particularly good for snacking on and you will find that many restaurants provide them as an alternative to bread.

Egg Whites

The egg debate is an age-old one. Some people say the yolks are fine to eat, others say they are not okay to eat and that you should only eat egg whites. Whole eggs are a fantastic source of protein and the biggest debate rages around the cholesterol and fat levels in the yolks. If you want to be safe, eat the whites on and start adding yolks back in at a later date.

Grapefruit

Grapefruits are an excellent fat burning food and this is being proved with more research every year. Grapefruit helps to kick start the digestive system, making fat burning an easier and more efficient process. You can start with pure grapefruit juice if you want and work your way up to eating a grapefruit.

Chicken Breast

Chicken breast is a staple part of many diets, although it is obviously no good if you are going vegetarian or vegan. It is low in fat and high in protein and is far healthier to eat than the dark meat from a chicken. Do remember to take the skin off, as this is where all the fat is and use a variety of spices and herbs to boost the flavor. Combine eating chicken breast with strength training to help tone up your muscles, which will boost your metabolism rate as well.

Bananas

Bananas are one of the most natural foods to eat and are the subject of many research programs for their effect on weight loss. They are so easy to add in to your diet on a daily basis because they are such a versatile fruit. They can be eaten on their own, chopped up and added to oatmeal or yoghurt and are a great source of potassium, natural sugar and energy.

Pears

Pears are often dismissed from a diet but they really should be included. They are full of flavor, and contain a whole range of benefits, which are great for weight loss. They help you to feel fuller for longer and they are different in consistency to apples and other fruits, which makes their fiber content more effective than others are. They can be eaten as they are, chopped up or cooked.

Pine Nuts

Pine nuts include a phytonutrient that can help to suppress the appetite, which means you can ditch the cost of buying expensive diet pills that are full of chemicals to do the same thing. They are tiny and they are crunchy so you can eat a lot without worrying about the effect of them and without ruining your weight loss efforts. These are one food you can binge on without any trouble.

Mushrooms

You won't see the benefits if you switch pepperoni for mushrooms on your next pizza but if you start increasing the amount you are eating, along with a range of other healthier foods, you will see a difference, because they are low in calories and high in vitamins. Don't be boring though; try all different ones from the supermarket and enjoy a range of textures, flavors and other great benefits.

Lentils

Lentils are another food that is gaining in popularity and are not just for a vegetarian diet. They contain fiber, which helps your digestive system keep your blood sugar from spiking and help you to feel fuller for longer. They are also full of protein and help to keep cholesterol levels down as well as helping the body to process carbohydrates better.

Hot Peppers

Jalapenos, chipotles and habaneros peppers are excellent weight loss foods while adding a healthy kick to the flavor of a dish.

Instead of ruining your stomach lining like some believe, these will actually help to protect your stomach and prevent ulcers by killing off the bad bacteria.

Broccoli

Broccoli is one of the best superfoods. Not only are they full of anti-oxidants, they are also jam packed with nutrients and fiber. They fill you up quickly and keep your digestive system clear which makes you feel so much better. Add spices or peppers to it to give it more flavor. Broccoli with a sprinkling of turmeric has been proven to keep prostate cancer at bay as well as help you lose weight.

Organic Lean Meats

Lean meats contain all of the protein you need without the fat levels but, if you are looking to lose weight, go for organic meats. With normal meats, the animals are pumped full of growth hormones, antibiotics and other nasty things which all end up in what you get on your plate and can slow down your weight loss. Organic meat do not contain any more nutrients than normal meat but this is a case of what it doesn't contain that makes it better. If organic is not n supply, look for grass-fed or all-natural brands.

Cantaloupe Melon

There are those who say that eating a cantaloupe burns off more calories than it contains but that is still up for debate. Whatever the outcome, it is a great food for helping to lose weight because, while it is sweet, it is low in calories, contains fiber and helps keep you moving. It is good on its own, in a fruit salad or even in a smoothie with other fruits and vegetables. Cantaloupe melon can also help to keep your skin looking great.

Spinach

Spinach is so often left lying on the plate but it is a fantastic food for health and weight loss. It is full of antioxidants, vitamins and minerals and is good to eat in a number of ways. Cook it, eat it raw in a salad, however you want. It adds bulk without adding calories. Try to go for organic and buy in bulk if you buy fresh because you can freeze it for a later date.

Green Tea

Green tea is full of antioxidants and can help you to burn off fat. This is because green tea contains catechins, which help your body to start burning off more calories and well as fat. It isn't processed like so many other teas, and is packed with antioxidants and phytonutrients that make it one of the superstar super foods.

Cinnamon

Cinnamon is one of the most powerful spices and is no longer just used for cooking. Instead, you can get the benefits from cinnamon by adding a teaspoon a day into your diet. It works by regulating your blood sugar levels, which also plays a big part in the way you are feeling throughout the day. Low blood sugar levels are indicated by a sluggish heavy feeling. Keeping your sugar levels even can also help to stop cravings. One good way is to have a drink of honey and cinnamon in hot water every day.

Asparagus

Asparagus plays a big role in weight loss with lots of different benefits and each benefit plays a specific role in weight loss. Asparagus helps to eliminate toxins from the body, helps with the digestion process and leaves the good bacteria thriving in your gut. It also has loads of vitamins, minerals and antioxidants. It tastes nice and can also be boosted with spices and seasonings.

Avocado

Avocado is a great slimming aid and contain loads of healthy fats. They were avoided for a long time because of that fat content, at a time when fat was given the label of being evil but we now know that not all fats are bad and that god fats can help to burn fat. Add avocado to salads, sandwiches, eat them as they are or make your own guacamole with them.

Peanut Butter

Peanut butter contains good fats that help to burn fat but do go for organic peanut butter as it doesn't contain any of them extra salt and sugar and tat standard peanut butter contains. It can be eaten as part of a smoothie or a piece of celery dipped in peanut butter makes a great filling snack. You can also have almond butter but it is more expensive.

Salmon

Salmon, like other fish, contains a high level of omega 3 and this is one thing that is sorely lacking in many diets today. It may be classed as a fatty fish but it is not high in saturated fats, which are the bad fats and the omega 3 content makes it better than anything else. You would need to add this in gradually to see how your body takes to it so start with once a week. If you get on with it, increase that and look around for some great tasting salmon recipes.

Apple Cider Vinegar

Go for raw organic apple cider vinegar because it contains enzymes that help your digestive system and can help with weight loss over time. The recommended way is to add it to filtered or distilled water and drink it before you eat; this helps your food to be properly digested so that your body gets all the goodness from the nutrients instead of wasting them. It can also help suppress the appetite so drink it if you find yourself hungry between meals.

Greek Yoghurt

Greek yoghurt is healthier than any other yoghurt because it is full of proteins and has a lower sugar content than normal yoghurt. You don't have to use it as a substitute for normal yoghurt though; you can use it in place of sour cream, cutting down fat and calories and you can also experiment with baking, using it in place of other fats and oils. This could take a bit of trial and error to get it right though.

Olive Oil

Olive oil is a much healthier oil than vegetable or seed oils and it can be used in a variety of ways. Not only can you add it to salads, either on its own or as part of a salad dressing, you can also use it for cooking in.

Blueberries

Blueberries are excellent for fat loss, not just weight. They help to break down sugars and fats in the body as well as tasting amazing. You can use them to add flavor to any meal and they also go well with other fruits – just skip the cream and sugar! Add them to yoghurt or oatmeal for a tasty breakfast or snack.

Turkey Breast

Turkey breast is good for those moments when you are hungry and feel as though you are going to cave in. It is a good source of lean protein and is popular on low or no carb diets. It is a god meat to eat if you are strength training and building up muscle, as well as being able to boost your metabolism.

Flax Seeds

Flax seed can be sprinkled on just about anything you want and it is a better option than sugar. It contains healthy doses of fiber, omega 3 and helps to keep you feeling fuller for longer. The essential fatty acids contained in flax seed helps to boost metabolism and lower bad cholesterol levels.

Use Fresh and Organic

Use fresh ingredients wherever possible and stick to organic. Processed foods are lower in antioxidants and have little weight loss power left in them. Organic foods are best because they don't contain the chemicals and have not been genetically modified.

You can make soups and smoothies out of some of the ingredients on this list and this is a great way to get the benefits without eating a plate of raw food. Soup is excellent for weight loss and is helps with the digestion process and you can put lots of different foods together in the same soup for a real fat busting meal that is packed full of vitamins. You can have the soup as a starter or as a meal on its own. It is also much easier to digest than some foods.

Chapter 4 - The Top 20 Superfoods You Should be Eating

Everyone wants to be healthy and fit. There are many ways to stay healthy and fit, but all of them circle back to two things: exercise and diet. Nowadays, people find it difficult to follow a diet routine and an exercise regime. But if you want to stay healthy, there are no alternatives to these two options. Almost every day, we are introduced to a new form of exercise or diet routine. One such new (but really old) introduction to the world of diet is 'superfoods.'

Superfoods have become really popular nowadays thanks to the publicity they have received in recent times. There are many types of superfoods, most of them being plant-based, but there are also many superfoods that are dairy or fish-based. All these foods contain high amounts of nutrients. Some commonly found superfoods include salmon, kale, apples, blueberries, etc.

There exists no specific definition of superfoods. They are not a separate food group. Rather, superfoods are foods that contain high amounts of nutrients and are generally good for the health of your heart. Most of the superfoods contain a variety of nutrients, including protein, fats, vitamins, and essential minerals. They also contain many different antioxidants, which make them effective against cancer and similar diseases.

Many superfoods also contain a high amount of healthy fats, which are great for the health of your heart. They are also good for the health of your cardiovascular system. Many superfoods are also effective against digestive problems as well. They contain high amounts of phytochemicals that have many health benefits. Phytochemicals provide foods their deep color and taste. Adding superfoods to your day-to-day diet can help you a lot. It can bring in a lot of positive changes in your lifestyle. It can help you become fit and healthy.

In this chapter, let us have a look at twenty important superfoods that you can incorporate into your daily meals. Almost all of these superfoods are easily available on the market. Most of them are quite affordable. They are also versatile, and you can make a variety of recipes with them.

Broccoli

Broccoli is considered to be one of the healthiest vegetables as it is packed with nutrients. It contains a high amount of fiber and is rich in antioxidants as well. These properties of broccoli allow it to fight cancer. Its high antioxidant content is good for the repair of body cells and tissues. It also contains high amounts of minerals and vitamins. Broccoli is also great for the cardiovascular system and immune system. It has anti-inflammatory properties, which makes it an overall healthy vegetable. Along with its high fiber content, it is low in fats, which makes it best for people who are trying to lose weight.

Broccoli, along with other cruciferous vegetables, can reduce the growth of cancer cells. Broccoli can also reduce the blood sugar levels and is thus a boon for diabetics. Broccoli can also prevent (and reduce) cardiovascular tissue damage.

As said above, broccoli contains a high amount of fiber, which is great for digestive health. It makes bowel movements regular and smooth. Dark green vegetables such as broccoli contain a lot of nutrients that can prevent the signs of aging. One such nutrient is sulforaphane. Sulforaphane is also good for the health of the brain.

Broccoli contains a high amount of vitamin C. Vitamin C is good for the immune system. It is also good for oral health and can keep your teeth healthy. Broccoli is also good for your bones as it contains high amounts of phosphorous, calcium, and vitamin K. According to some studies, broccoli can even control joint disorders.

Broccoli is a highly recommended food for pregnant or lactating women. Broccoli is rich in nutrients, which ensures the healthy development of the fetus. It helps lactating women stay healthy. It is high in folate, which is great for the health of new mothers.

Broccoli can also control inflammation and boost immune power. It can also regulate blood sugar levels. Thus it is clear that broccoli is a superfood that can help you get healthy and fit. There are various ways of consuming broccoli. To avoid repetition, use different methods every time you cook broccoli.

Avocado

Avocado is a green, pear-shaped fruit that is often referred to as an "alligator pear." It is prized for its healthy fats, fiber, and various important nutrients. There are many types of avocado that vary in shape and color — from pear-shaped to round and green to black.

Avocados have become a highly popular food and ingredient today. They are consumed in a variety of forms and are often the main ingredient in salads, dips, shakes, etc. They are rich in vitamins- especially vitamin B, potassium, and folic acid. Another aspect that makes avocados great for health is that it allows the body to absorb nutrients effectively. This means that avocados help you to absorb the nutrients provided by other food in a more efficient manner. This is especially true in the case of carotenoids, which is an essential cancer-fighting compound.

Avocados contain high amounts of monounsaturated fatty acids, such as oleic acids. This allows them to control and manage cholesterol levels. Oleic acid is also good for preventing breast cancer.

Avocados are full of potassium, which is good for the health of the heart and bones. It can prevent many heart diseases and disorders and can also prevent stroke. It is also good for digestion and is often used for 'detox' process. Along with potassium, avocados also contain high amounts of vitamin C, B6, and D, along with manganese, and riboflavin. All these components work together to improve your immune system. They are also a good source of vitamins A and E, which can prevent cancer to a certain extent.

Another aspect that makes avocados great is that they are rich in omega-3. It reduces the risk of heart diseases and disorder and is good for your arteries. They also contain high amounts of lecithin, a type of fatty acid that is crucial for healthy nervous tissues.

Avocados are full of fiber as well. Fiber is essential for digestive health, and it can also help you lose weight. Fiber satiates you and thus prevents you from eating unnecessary and empty calories. According to various surveys, people who eat avocados regularly are comparatively healthier than those who don't. They also have a lower risk of developing metabolic diseases. Avocados contain high amounts of lutein and zeaxanthin. These antioxidants are good for the health of your eyes and optic nerves. They can also help you prevent cataract and macular degeneration.

Avocados are great for people who want to lose weight. It can help you keep full for a long time. Avocados are low in carbs and thus can help you lose weight efficiently. Incorporating avocados in your daily diet is easy as it is tasty and easy to use. You can use avocados in various forms, including avocado butter, shakes, salad, toast, etc.

Sweet Potato

Sweet potato is a delicious and nutrient-rich vegetable that is known for its distinctive sweet flavor. It is a highly versatile and healthful vegetable that is readily available in the market. Although people confuse sweet potato with yam all the time, both of them are different. Sweet potato is one of the most easily available and nutrient-rich superfoods. It contains high amounts of beta-carotene, which is a great antioxidant.

Sweet potato also contains high amounts of vitamin A. This vitamin is essential for the health of our bones, skin, immune system, eyes, and reproductive system as well. Sweet potato also has nutrients that can help you prevent cancer. It also contains high amounts of vitamin C, which is great for people who have asthma or arthritis. It can also help people who have diabetes as it has a very low glycemic index, which means it does not have a significant effect on blood glucose levels.

As said above, sweet potato is sweet in taste and is a starchy root vegetable that is grown all around the globe. This tube is available in various sizes, shapes, and colors. They contain high amounts of fiber, which makes them a great food for people who are trying to lose weight. They also increase the number of good gut bacteria that is good for the digestive system.

Sweet potatoes contain high amounts of different antioxidants. These antioxidants are helpful against various types of cancers. For instance, sweet potato contains anthocyanin, an antioxidant that is well known for slowing down the growth of cancerous cells of cancers affecting bladder, colon, breast, and the stomach. Sweet potatoes are also a rich source of beta-carotene, which is good for optical health.

Sweet potatoes are extremely versatile and can be used like regular potatoes. There are many different ways of cooking sweet potatoes. They can be boiled, roasted, baked, fried pan-cooked, or steamed. It is possible to consume them with skin or without skin as well. If you like eating chips, try eating sweet potato chips. These chips are healthier than regular chips. As sweet potatoes are naturally sweet, they go well with many different flavors. You can make sweet as well as savory dishes with sweet potatoes.

Wheat Grass

Wheatgrass is a superfood made out of the Triticum Aestivum plant. It contains high amounts of nutrients that are great for your health. It is generally consumed in the form of fresh juice, but nowadays, it is also available in the form of powder. The powder is far more convenient than the juice. While a lot of people now understand the importance of wheatgrass, many people are still unaware of its benefits, which is why it still remains an underrated superfood. If consumed daily, wheatgrass can help you tackle many diseases and disorders.

As said above, wheatgrass is full of a variety of nutrients that are necessary for our body. Wheatgrass also has many nourishing and therapeutic properties. It contains many different vitamins and minerals that keep fit and active. It also contains a variety of enzymes that are good for your digestive system. Another factor that makes wheatgrass really great is that it improves and enhances the immune system. It is also good for people who are trying to lose weight because it tackles cholesterol levels and minimizes them. Wheatgrass also makes you calm and relaxed. It can relieve you of anxiety. It improves mental function. It reduces stress. It improves cognitive function and can also be used to prevent the symptoms of Alzheimer's disease.

Salmon

Salmon is a highly nutritious fish that is considered to be an important superfood. It contains high amounts of omega three and healthy fats. The nutrients and oil present in salmon are rarely found in other species of fish, which makes salmon one of the healthiest fish. Salmon contains a high amount of polyunsaturated fats. These fats reduce the levels of serum triglycerides and can enhance brain functioning and cardiovascular health as well.

It is true that salmon is a pricey seafood option, but the number of nutrients (and taste) present in it makes it worth it. It considered being the best source of dietary omega 3. Other, considerably cost-effective fish such as herring roe and sardines too contain omega-3, but salmon contain the highest amounts.

Fish is a really good source of omega 3 as they provide long-chain polyunsaturated fatty acids. These acids are as follows: Eicosapentaenoic and docosahexaenoic acid (EPA and DHA).

Such combinations are only found in seafood and marine algae or seaweed. Terrain plants provide short-chain omega-3 alpha-linolenic acid (ALA). The human body can utilize ALA to synthesize EPA and DHA, but getting them directly from the source is always better as it reduces the work and energy required. For instance, one 4 oz portion of cooked salmon can provide approximately 2000 mg of omega-3s.

The human body needs L-tryptophan (an amino acid) to make melatonin. This acid is found in abundance in salmon. This is why people who eat salmon regularly rarely face any sleep-related problems. A 4 oz serving of salmon contains approximately 250–400 mg of L-tryptophan.

The vitamin B family is necessary for the body as these vitamins are used to regulate energy metabolism and enhance tissue formation as well. Salmon contains a lot of vitamin Bs, including B2, B3, B6, and B12. If you are a pescatarian, then eating salmon is one of the best ways to get vitamin B12. A 4 oz piece of salmon contains 5.7 mcg of B12 or 236% of the recommended daily intake.

Salmon also contains high amounts of minerals, such as phosphorus and calcium. These minerals are good for the health of your teeth and bones. It also contains other trace materials such as selenium, which is a great antioxidant. A 4 oz serving of salmon provides 365 mg of phosphorus or 52% of the recommended daily intake.

Salmon is also a great source of protein. Salmon contains various amino acids that are essential for the health of your body. It also contains proteins such as calcitonin, which promotes healthy joints and bones.

Astaxanthin is another antioxidant that is found in abundance in salmon and similar seafood. It is a fat-soluble pigment that is red in color; this is why salmon looks so red. It also contains high amounts of carotenoids that can reduce the number of free radicals. This is why salmon is considered to be one of the best superfoods.

Pomegranate Seeds

Pomegranate is considered to be one of the best superfoods currently available. It has been used since ancient times in the Middle East and has been celebrated for its taste and health benefits. The outer skin of the pomegranate is tough, but the insides are juicy, delicious, and blood red.

The seeds of pomegranate are slightly tart and sweet. These seeds not only help you stay healthy but also free of disease. They are a great addition to your salads as they will not only make it more colorful and healthy, but it will make your salads tasty as well.

As said earlier, pomegranates were used in Asia, India, Africa, and the Mediterranean since ancient times. In ancient times, pomegranates were used to denote fertility. It is one of the most represented fruits in art throughout the centuries.

Pomegranate was introduced to North America around a few centuries ago. It is now grown in abundance in parts of Arizona and California. All the parts of pomegranates contain immense amounts of nutrients. This is why pomegranates have become such a rage in the world of superfoods. Nowadays, pomegranates are easily available in the market in the form of juices, extracts, powders, supplements, etc. The fruits are available in abundance in supermarkets.

Nilumin...

Pomegranates can help you lower cholesterol, which makes them great for cardiovascular and heart diseases. Pomegranates also contain high amounts of vitamin C, which provides them immense anti-inflammatory properties. Pomegranates are also potent against certain cancers and Type 2 diabetes as well. Pomegranates also contain high amounts of antioxidants, which can help to reduce high blood pressure. Pomegranate is also good for the health of your brain, arteries, and heart.

According to certain studies, if you consume around 8 oz of pomegranate juice daily, it can work wonders for your health. Pomegranate is also good for 'masculine health.' It can improve erections and can also slow down the growth of prostate cancer cells as well.

Blueberries

Blueberries are versatile fruits that can be either eaten raw and fresh or can be utilized in a variety of recipes as well. Blueberries can be used fresh or can be eaten frozen as well.

Blueberries contain high amounts of anthocyanin. This compound gives them a distinct color. It is also responsible for its numerous health benefits. Blueberries are good for the health of your heart. They are also good for your skin, hair, blood pressure, bone strength, diabetes, mental health, and cancer. One cup of blueberries can provide you with 24% of the daily total vitamin C requirement.

As said above, blueberries are exceptionally versatile, and they can be used in a variety of forms and in a variety of recipes as well. For instance, blueberries are often used to top salads, ice cream, yogurt, shakes, pancakes, cereals, oatmeal, and salads too. They can also be blended into syrups and smoothies. You

can also add them to sweetbreads and muffins. You can make a variety of desserts with blueberries.

Blueberries also contain high amounts of vitamin K. This is why people who are on blood thinners should avoid using a lot of blueberries or should consult their health professional before eating a lot of blueberries.

Blueberries contain many different flavonoids. Flavonoids are antioxidants that have multiple health benefits.

Eating a variety of fruits and vegetables is one of the best ways to stay healthy and tackle diseases and disorders. For instance, a lot of studies have proved the consuming blueberries can help you tackle obesity, heart problems, diabetes, and various other diseases as well. Blueberries can improve your overall health. Blueberries are also good for people who are trying to lose weight. They are also good for the health of your skin and hair.

Blueberries are often sold frozen. While freezing them ensures a long shelf life, the process removes many essential nutrients. According to a study, the amount of anthocyanin in frozen blueberries decreases rapidly, and in a couple of months, it can go down by 30-40 %. More research is required regarding this. But it is always better to buy and eat fresh blueberries whenever you can. Try to find organic berries.

Blueberries contain a variety of minerals as well. For instance, they are rich in calcium, phosphorus, iron, magnesium, zinc, manganese, and vitamin K. All these nutrients are good for the health of your bones. If you consume adequate amounts of vitamins and minerals, your bones become healthy and non-brittle. Iron and zinc are responsible for the health of your joints. Vitamin K deficiency often leads to brittle bones. This is because vitamin K improves the absorption of calcium. A low amount of vitamin K ultimately leads to a low amount of calcium.

Collagen is essential for the health of our skin. It keeps it tight, young, fresh, and healthy. Collagen needs a lot of vitamin C to perform properly. Collagen also protects the skin from various damaging factors such as pollution, the sun, and smoke. Blueberries contain high amounts of vitamin C, which enhances the potency of collagen. Thus, blueberries can help you achieve beautiful and attractive looking skin.

Blueberries contain no sodium. Excessive sodium is bad for your health, especially for your blood pressure. On the other hand, blueberries are full of calcium, potassium, and magnesium. The deficiency of these minerals can often lead to high blood pressure. Thus, blueberries can help you regulate your blood pressure.

A high fiber diet is recommended for people who have Type 1 diabetes. A high fiber diet can help to lower blood glucose levels. Similarly, people suffering from Type 2 diabetes can also benefit a lot from consuming a high fiber diet. A single cup of blueberries contains around 3.6 grams of fiber.

Blueberries are also good for the health of your heart. They contain high amounts of potassium, fiber, folate, vitamin B6, vitamin C, and phytonutrients. All these nutrients are essential for the health of your heart. Blueberries contain no cholesterol. The fiber in blueberries can reduce the amount of cholesterol present in the body already.

Homocysteine is a harmful chemical that is present in our body. A lot of homocysteine can lead to clogging and damaging blood vessels. It is extremely dangerous for the health of or heart.

Blueberries contain a high amount of vitamin B6 and folate, which can prevent the buildup of homocysteine.

According to a study, it was found that women who consumed around three servings of blueberries every week showed a reduced risk of heart diseases and disorders. The various vitamins present in blueberries act as antioxidants that can tackle free radicals present in the body.

According to research, antioxidants can also prevent the growth of tumors and reduce inflammation. They can slow down the growth of cancer cells in the lungs, esophagus, mouth, pharynx, pancreas, colon, and prostate. They can also prevent endometrial cancer, as well.

Blueberries are rich in folate. Folate plays a crucial role in the repair and synthesis of DNA. Due to this, the DNA does not mutate. DNA mutations are often responsible for cancer.

Blueberries can also tackle cognitive damage, especially in women. Similar studies have proved how blueberries can improve memory and coordination. It can also help to prevent and tackle other brain-related problems.

Blueberries are also great against constipation. They are good for the health of your digestive system. They contain lots of fiber, which is good for digestion. Dietary fiber is also good for weight loss and weight management. High fiber foods lead to early satiation. This way, you do not end up consuming a lot of empty calories, making blueberries a miracle berry!

Quinoa

Quinoa has become a rage in the world of fitness and health now. Quinoa is considered one of the healthiest and nutrient-rich foods available in the market. It is a highly healthy and delicious food. It is a highly versatile and incredible food that is a great source of carbs. Many people believe that quinoa is a grain just like rice or wheat, but it is quite different than them. In fact, quinoa is not a grain at all. It is known as pseudo-grain. It is a form of seed that is highly nutritious.

Quinoa is one of the most nutrient-dense carbs available today. It has around six grams of proteins per cup. It is also the only carb source that contains all nine essential amino acids. Along with this, quinoa is a complete protein. It also contains a high amount of lysine. Lysine is an amino acid that is necessary for healing and repairing muscles. This is why many gym rats generally include quinoa in their diet.

Quinoa also has many other benefits, such as it is full of various minerals and vitamins. It is a rich source of copper, iron, phosphorus, and manganese. Manganese and copper control free radicals and are good for the health of bones and teeth. Phosphorous and iron play an integral role in the creation of energy. Then it can also help against the development of cancer cells. Another point that makes quinoa really great is that it is full of fiber. Each serving contains around 2.5 grams of fiber. Fiber is great for people who are trying to lose weight. It satiates you and keeps you feeling full for a long time. This way, you do not consume random, useless calories. Fiber is also good for the health of your digestive tract. It is also good for diabetics as it improves the function of insulin.

Nowadays, there are many different recipes of quinoa available online. While North America is trying to grow quinoa locally, a lot of quinoa is still imported from South America. Due to the increasing demands of quinoa, it has become a priced commodity. But the price is definitely worth the health benefits of the product. This is why people are still buying quinoa in abundance.

Nowadays, quinoa is available in a variety of forms. For instance, you can now buy quinoa cereal, pasta, flour, cookies, etc. It is an extremely versatile food product and can be used in a variety of recipes. You can make delicious desserts, cookies, granola bars, cakes, side dishes, breakfast foods, shakes, etc. from quinoa. It is easy to use, which is why many people now try to incorporate it into their daily meals.

Quinoa is a boon for people who are allergic to gluten. It contains no gluten and is thus great for people who are on a no-gluten diet. Gluten is found in many essential grains such as rye, oats, wheat, and barley, which make them unsuitable for anyone who has celiac disease or is allergic to gluten. Quinoa is rich in nutrients and contains no gluten, which has made it really popular with the gluten-free community.

Quinoa has a slightly nutty flavor that is not at all overpowering and goes well with almost everything. It is easy to cook, and it hardly takes more than 12-15 minutes to get done. It is also popular with kids in the form of cereal and cookies.

Almonds

Almonds are not only tasty, but they are also full of nutrients. They contain high amounts of minerals, proteins, vitamins, fiber, etc. Their nutrition makes them a really healthy superfood. For instance, only a handful of almonds contain around 1/8th of our daily protein needs. Almonds are versatile, and there are multiple ways to eat them. You can eat them raw, or you can also toast them. They are often added to sweet as well as savory dishes as toppings or garnish. They are a great addition to salads as they provide a good crunch to it. Nowadays, almonds are available in a variety of forms, including chopped almonds, peeled almonds, slivered almonds, sliced almonds, almond flakes, almond flour, almond oil, almond milk, and almond butter. Almond is known as a nut, but it is actually a seed full of nutrients.

Almond trees are one of the earliest plants that human beings cultivated. Archaeologists have found evidence showcasing that people in Jordan domesticated almond trees around 5000 years ago. Almonds are full of fats, but they are full of unsaturated fats. Unsaturated fats are healthy and essential for the body. They do not increase LDL or low-density lipoprotein. LDL is often known as "bad" cholesterol.

According to the AHA or American Heart Association, moderate amounts of unsaturated fats can improve your cholesterol levels. Almonds contain no cholesterol. According to a study published in 2005 says that almonds also contain high amounts of vitamin E. Vitamin E is an essential antioxidant that can stop the oxidization process that is responsible for the clogging of arteries. Along with this, another study conducted in 2018 found the same results. According to this study, almonds can help to increase or maintain the levels of HDL or high-density lipoprotein or "good" cholesterol. According to this study, people are recommended to consume at least 45 grams of almonds a day for cardiovascular health.

According to a 2015 study, almonds can help against cancer as well. The study says that almonds can reduce the risk of breast cancer by about two to three times. Peanuts and walnuts, too, were found to be helpful against breast cancer.

In another study conducted in 2011, around 20 people suffering from Type 2 diabetes were observed. They were asked to eat 60 g of almonds every day for 12 weeks. It was found that the almonds improved their blood lipids, blood sugar levels, and fat levels as well.

One oz of almonds contains around 76. 5 mg of magnesium on average. This is around 20-24% of the total daily requirement of a healthy adult. While magnesium supplements are a great way to tackle deficiency, healthy people can eat almonds to avoid becoming deficient.

Almonds contain high amounts of fibers, proteins, and healthy fats. They are low in carbs. These factors make them great for people who are trying to lose weight. According to a study conducted in 2015, people who eat almonds as morning snacks eat fewer calories throughout the day. This is because almonds contain fiber, which helps you stay satiated for a long time. This is why almonds are often a staple ingredient of breakfast cereals and muesli.

Almonds are also a rich source of vitamin K, manganese, calcium, copper, zinc, and protein. All these are responsible for good and healthy bones.

Beet Roots

Beetroot is a delicious, healthy, and great looking vegetable that is packed with nutrients. Beet leaves are healthy as well. Beetroot has been used since ancient times for various medical purposes. For instance, it was once upon a time used to treat fevers, skin issues, constipation, etc.

Beetroot contains high amounts of folate and iron. Folate is naturally occurring folic acid, which is good for your health. It also contains high amounts of magnesium, nitrates, betaine, betacyanin, and many other antioxidants that are good for health. According to recent studies, it has been proven that beetroots can also help to lower blood pressure and can prevent dementia as well. It is great for gym rats as it increases stamina.

As said above, beetroot contains high amounts of nitrates. Nitrates are converted into nitric oxide by our bodies. This chemical can lower blood pressure. According to studies, beetroot can moderately control blood pressure; however, more study is necessary. It is still considered to be great for the health of your heart and cardiovascular system.

Another study conducted in 2013 showed the relation between beetroots and improved exercise and performance. According to this study, beetroot can improve activity inactive as well as inactive individuals. But elite athletes showed little to no change.

According to a study conducted in 2010, beetroot juice can enhance the flow of blood in the brain. It is also good for the skin and hair and has many cosmetic benefits.

Beetroot has a distinct color and flavor. It is recommended to consume it raw, but you can also cook it according to the recipe. It is a great addition to salads as it provides taste, color, and crunch. Beetroot juice is another common form in which beetroot can be consumed with ease.

Kale

Kale is considered one of the healthiest leafy vegetables. It contains high amounts of nutrients and is really great for people who are trying to lose weight. Kale contains many medicinal properties as well. Kale is highly versatile, and it can be had in many different forms. It is easy to incorporate in daily meals. It can be eaten raw, fried, or it can be made into soups and salads as well. Thus, kale is one of the best superfoods currently available.

Kale is a member of the cabbage family. Like other cruciferous vegetables, such as broccoli, Brussels sprouts, and cauliflower, kale too is extremely healthy and nutritious. There are many different varieties of kale available in the market. Green and purple varieties are the most popular. The shape of leaves of kale varieties varies a lot. Some have plain leaves, while others have curved and rounded leaves. Curly Kale or Scots Kale is a popular variety of kale that has curly leaves and a stark green color.

Kale is extremely rich in nutrients. A single cup contains high amounts of minerals such as calcium, manganese, potassium, copper, and magnesium. It also contains high amounts of vitamins such as A, K, C, B6. A single cup of kale contains around 6 grams of carbs, 3 grams of proteins, and only 33 calories. Kale contains little to no fat, which makes it great for people who are trying to lose weight. Kale is considered to be one of the most nutrient-dense foods in the world.

Kale is rich in antioxidants like other green leafy vegetables. It contains high amounts of beta-carotene, Quercetin, and Kaempferol. It also contains high amounts of vitamin C, which is good for your immune system. In fact, a cup of kale contains more vitamin C than an orange!

Kale contains high amounts of bile acids, such as sequestrants, which can control your cholesterol level. Thus, kale is really great for the health of your heart and cardiovascular system as well.

Cancer is an extremely terrible disease that can wreak havoc in a person's life. Kale contains many components that can fight cancer efficiently.

Kale contains high amounts of minerals and can thus prevent mineral deficiency. Spinach is another green leafy vegetable that is full of nutrients, but when compared to kale, spinach falls short. Kale is not only rich in minerals, but it is also low in oxalate.

People who are trying to lose weight are often worried about their diet and what to eat and what not to eat. Kale is definitely a great choice for anyone who is trying to lose weight. It is low in calories but can still keep you satiated for a long time.

Spinach

Spinach is a great leafy vegetable that contains high amounts of nutrients. It is dark, leafy, and contains very few calories. It is good for your skin, bones, hair, and heart. It also contains high amounts of iron, protein, minerals, and vitamins. Spinach can help you to control blood sugar levels, improve bone health, and can also lower the risk of cancer significantly. It also contains a variety of minerals that are good for your health.

Spinach has been used by many different cultures since ancient times. It is a staple food of middle-eastern, Mediterranean, and Southeast Asian cultures. It is versatile and can be added to almost any food. It has its own distinct flavor, but it is not overpowering and thus can be mixed with other ingredients with ease. Spinach is also cheap and easy to cook. There are many different ways of cooking spinach, but you can also eat it raw. Spinach is really good for reducing oxidative stress. It is also good for blood pressure levels and optical health as well.

Spinach contains high amounts of insoluble fiber, which is good for weight loss and digestion. It also contains high amounts of lutein, kaempferol, quercetin, nitrates, and zeaxanthin, which are all good for your health.

Spinach contains high amounts of vitamin K1, so people who suffer from kidney stones should avoid it. It is also not recommended for people who are on blood thinners. Other than these people, everyone can consume spinach.

Green Tea

Green tea is a great beverage that contains many different nutrients. It has many health benefits and properties due to the way it is prepared and processed. To make black tea, the tea leaves are fermented, which gives it a distinct taste and color. In the case of green tea, the leaves are steamed. Due to this, the tea leaves do not lose a lot of nutrients and taste. This is why green tea is extremely rich in antioxidants.

Green tea is known to prevent or slow down the growth of cancer. It fights the battle against cancer on all fronts. For instance, it protects the DNA against any damage. It also attacks the cancerous cells. It can even shut down crucial molecules that are responsible for the development of cancer.

Nicholas Bjorn

According to recent Swedish research, green tea also stops the formation of new blood vessels. These vessels are responsible for spreading tumors.

Green tea can also reduce and repair the damage caused to the liver due to alcohol. It is also good against various diseases, including Parkinson's and rheumatoid arthritis. It also prevents cholesterol from choking blood vessels. Women who drink green tea regularly have better bones than those who don't. Thus, green tea also reduces the risk of osteoporosis in women.

Green tea is full of nutrients, such as antioxidants that are great for the body. These are responsible for enhanced brain function, reduced risk of cancer, and enhanced fat loss as well.

Green tea also contains small amounts of caffeine that can keep you awake for a long time. It also acts as a stimulant and is good for the health of your brain. While the amount of caffeine present in green tea is lower than the amount present in coffee, it is still potent enough to give you efficient results.

Green tea also contains important amino acids, such as L-theanine. This amino acid works in combination with caffeine to improve brain function. Green tea can also boost your metabolism and thus can lead to efficient fat burning. It has other antioxidants that can help you prevent cancer.

There are various bioactive compounds present in green tea, which are good for the health of your brain. They can reduce the effects of Parkinson's and Alzheimer's effectively. These two are the most common neurodegenerative disorders. Green tea contains a high amount of catechins, which can reduce the growth of certain viruses and bacteria. This is turn can reduce infections and can also improve your oral and dental health. It is also effective against halitosis.

In certain controlled trials, it was observed that green tea could also reduce blood sugar levels and thus can reduce the risk of Type 2 diabetes as well. Green tea can also reduce LDL cholesterol. Thus, green tea can help you live longer and look young for a long time as well.

Apples

Apples are one of the best fruits, as they contain no cholesterol or fats. They also contain no sodium and are a great low-calorie snack. Apples are not only delicious, but they are also highly nutritious. Apples contain high amounts of dietary fiber. It is estimated that one medium-sized fruit contains around 5 grams of dietary fiber. Apples are a rich source of soluble fiber, which is good for satiation. This is why apples are often an integral part of the diet of people who are trying to lose weight. Apples keep you feeling full for a long time.

Apples contain high amounts of vitamin C along with fiber. They are also a rich source of polyphenols. Polyphenols have multiple health benefits and are great for your cardiovascular health. Apples also contain nutrients that can help you to lower your cholesterol levels. According to studies, eating apples regularly can also help you lower the risk of Type 2 diabetes.

The type of fiber that is present in apple acts as food for bacteria. These good gut bacteria are essential for digestive health. They are also helpful in the case of heart problems, obesity, and Type 2 diabetes. Apples also contain many different nutrients that can fight cancer efficiently.

Apples also contain high amounts of anti-inflammatory compounds and antioxidants. They can help the regular immune system. These antioxidants are also good for the health of your bones. Apples are also great for your memory as they reduce wear and tear of neurotransmitters.

Flax Seeds

Flax seeds are tiny, but they contain high amounts of nutrients. They are full of omega-3, fiber, fatty acids, antioxidants, lignans, and many different varieties of vitamin B. Only a couple of teaspoons of flax seeds per day can provide you a lot of nutrients and can keep you healthy and fit. Incorporating flax seeds in your daily diet is easy as they can be added to literally any food, including salads, shakes, desserts, etc. Flax seeds and flaxseed oil have both been used for cooking for a long time. A lot of records regarding flax seeds have been found throughout the world.

Flax seeds come from the flowers of the flax plant. They are slightly larger than sesame seeds. They are normally available in shades such as dark brown and golden tan. They are flat and shiny. The seeds have a slightly nutty and earthy flavor, but their flavor often gets overpowered by other flavors when they are used in other dishes.

While flax seeds contain a multitude of nutrients, they are celebrated for being rich in lignans, omega 3, and fiber.

Flax seeds are great for vegetarians and vegans. Normally the best source for omega 3 is salmon, but vegans can get a lot of omega 3 from flaxseed. Flax seeds contain high amounts of ALA, which is a form of omega 3. ALA is good for the health of your heart, and it can also reduce the risk of stroke.

Along with ALA, flax seeds also contain high amounts of lignans. Lignans are a group of ingredients that are highly potent antioxidants. They can help to prevent breast and prostate cancer. They can also slow down the development of other cancers as well.

Flax seeds are great for people who suffer from digestive problems or are trying to lose weight. As flax seeds are full of fiber, they can improve your digestion. A high amount of fiber can also lower cholesterol and can improve the health of your heart as well. Flaxseeds also contain a high amount of insoluble fiber. Insoluble fiber can lower your blood sugar levels significantly — this why doctors often recommend diabetic patients to incorporate flax seeds in their diet.

Flax seeds are also great for people who are trying to lose weight. Flax seeds contain a high amount of fiber, which keeps you full for a long time.

Incorporating flax seeds into your diet is easy. You can either consume raw flax seeds or roasted flax seeds. The easiest way to eat flax seeds is by using them in shakes and salads. You can also consume spoonfuls of flax seeds twice daily. Flaxseed oil/gel is also great for the health of your hair and skin.

Oats

Oats have become really popular in modern times. They are high in nutrients that are available almost everywhere. They are extremely beneficial for our health. Oats are generally 100% whole grains that undergo a very low amount of processing. They contain high amounts of minerals, vitamins, and fiber. They also contain high amounts of beta-glucan. This is a soluble fiber that is good for lower cholesterol reabsorption. Oats also contain low amounts of sodium and a good amount of protein, which makes it great for people trying to lose weight.

According to the FDA review, oats can reduce LDLs, i.e., the lower serum cholesterol levels. This is a result of beta-glucan. This soluble fiber has made oats really popular among masses, especially among people who are trying to lose weight. While oats do help you to lose weight, they are not a 'one-time magic' solution that works instantly. You do need to combine oats with other methods of weight loss.

Oats are low in calories and contain high amounts of proteins and fiber. This makes them great for people trying to lose weight. They contain high amounts of potassium, magnesium, zinc, manganese, copper, thiamine, selenium, and pantothenic acid. They also contain high amounts of phytonutrients such as phytoestrogens, polyphenols, lignins, vitamin R, and protease inhibitors.

According to studies, if individuals who have high cholesterol consume even 3 grams of oat fiber every day (i.e., a bowl of oatmeal), their cholesterol levels can go down by 8-23 percent. Even a 1 percent drop is good for the heart and reduces the risk of developing heart disease. Thus, oats are really good for people who are at risk of developing heart problems.

Oats contain a lot of nutrients that make them exceptionally good for people who are trying to eat healthily and stay fit. They are good for your immune system and can help you tackle a lot of diseases and disorders as well. Oats are available with ease almost everywhere in the world. They are a staple ingredient in many baked goods. Almost all restaurants and breakfast places feature different kinds of oatmeal on their menu.

As said above, there are many different varieties of oats available in the market. Steel-cut oats can bring a lot of texture and flavor to otherwise plain and bland foods.

Oats are extremely versatile, and there are various methods of cooking and eating them. The easiest way to consume oats is in the form of cereals or oatmeal, but you can also consume oats in the form of cookies, cakes, shakes, salads, etc. Oats do not have a strong flavor profile and thus can be mixed with anything.

Hemp Seeds

It may come as a surprise, but it is true, hemp seeds are really good for your health. The scientific name of hemp seeds is Cannabis Sativa. Nowadays, thanks to research, people have realized that hemp seeds are indeed a superfood. They contain high amounts of nutrients that are really good for your body. Many people call hemp seeds to be the most nutritious food available for consumption. Hemp seeds are great for weight loss as they contain a high amount of fiber. They can help you stay full for a long time. They can also reduce your hunger pangs and thus ultimately control your weight. Eating hemp seeds is easy; just add a couple of teaspoons to your morning meal. Eating hemp seeds in the morning will help you stay satiated for a long time throughout the day.

Hemp seeds can be eaten raw, whole, toasted, or roasted. Nowadays, they are also available in various flavors to make them more palatable. You can use these seeds in various ways. You can also use the oil prepared from these seeds. The leftover stuff remaining after extracting oil from hemp seeds is quite nutrient-rich as well. Hemp is as healthy as any green vegetable. The health benefits of hemp and hemp seeds have now been proven by science as well.

Hemp seeds can efficiently reduce the risk of heart disease. Heart diseases and disorders are the two leading causes of death all around the world. According to research, hemp seeds can reduce the risk of developing heart diseases and disorders. Hemp seeds contain high amounts of amino acids. These acids produce nitric oxide in the body. This nitric oxide is good for the health of your blood vessels as it relaxes them and thus lowers and regulates your blood pressure. This, in turn, reduces the risk of heart disorders.

Omega 6, omega 3, and amino acids are essential for a healthy immune system. Hemp seeds are rich sources of these three nutrients and are thus great for your immune system. Amino acids are also good for the health of your skin. Hemp seed oil can work wonders for all your skin problems, including signs of aging, dark spots, acne, etc.

Hemp seeds are a boon for women suffering from menopause and PMS. It can effectively tackle the symptoms of PMS. According to studies, the hormone prolactin causes the symptoms associated with PMS. Hemp seeds contain a high amount of gamma linoleum acid, which can tackle prolactin by producing prostaglandin e1.

Hemp seeds also contain a high amount of fiber. They contain both insoluble and soluble fiber in an 80:20 ratio. This makes hemp seeds really good for your digestive health.

Hemp seeds do not contain any trans fats, which makes them great for people who are trying to lose weight. Thus, including hemp seeds in your regular diet will help you become fit, healthy, and young. If you do not like the taste of hemp seeds, try using the flavored ones.

Goji Berries

Goji berries have become one of the most celebrated superfoods now. They are reddish-orange berries that grow on the wolfberry plant. These plants are native to China. They are kind of tart but also have an inherent sweetness. Goji berries are more popular for their health benefits. They contain high amounts of antioxidants and a variety of nutrients as well.

Ancient Chinese medicine schools have been using goji berries for thousands of years for a variety of ailments and problems. Recently, goji berries and their immense health benefits have been introduced to the western world, which is why they have become a staple in health food stores.

Goji berries contain a high amount of vitamin C, even more than oranges. It also contains a high amount of selenium, calcium, iron, potassium, and zinc.

Goji berries also contain a high number of carotenoids, such as beta-carotene. It is good for the health of your eyes and optical nerves. It also contains a high amount of fiber, which is good for your digestive system. Goji berries can reduce fatigue and stress by giving your energy boosts. They contain a high amount of melatonin, which makes them great for people who suffer from insomnia or other sleep-related problems.

Goji berries are also rich in protein. They contain around 12-14% protein. They are the right combination of taste and health. In the west, these berries are generally available in dried form. High quality dried berries are soft and fleshy.

Goji berries are versatile, and there are many different ways you can use them. Some people prefer to eat them right out of the bag. They can also be mixed with other dried fruits, seeds, and nuts. You can also add them to smoothies and shakes. Some people also like to toss some berries in their salads. This makes the salad look and taste good.

Coconut

Coconut is a great superfood that can help you become fit and healthy. It is a versatile fruit that can be used in a variety of forms. Some of the most common forms include dried coconut, raw coconut meat, coconut oil, coconut water, coconut milk, etc. Coconuts have been grown and used since ancient times in various tropical regions around the world. Now they are gaining rapid popularity all over the world thanks to their immense culinary versatility and numerous health benefits.

While other fruits are full of carbs, coconut contains high amounts of fats. They are also a rich source of protein, vitamins, and minerals. Coconut contains a high amount of manganese, which is good for the health of your bones. It also metabolizes proteins, cholesterol, and carbs efficiently.

Coconuts are also rich in iron and copper. They also contain selenium. Selenium is an essential antioxidant that keeps your cells healthy.

Coconut contains high amounts of MCT or medium-chain triglycerides. Our body uses these fats for instant energy and does not store them. Thus, coconut is good for people who are trying to lose weight.

Coconut is also great for the health of your heart. It was found that people who live on Polynesian islands rarely get heart diseases and disorders. This is because their diet is rich in coconuts. According to certain studies, if you consume coconut oil, it may help you to reduce belly fat. This is especially great for people who are trying to lose weight. According to studies, coconut oil can also reduce cholesterol levels.

Coconut contains high amounts of fiber and fat but a low amount of carbs. This combination is great for your blood sugar levels. It can reduce your blood sugar levels efficiently.

Coconuts contain arginine. Arginine is an essential amino acid that improves pancreatic activity. It plays an important role in the regulation of blood sugar levels. Eating coconut also affects the beta cells present in the pancreas, which are responsible for the production of insulin.

Due to the high fiber content of coconut meat, you can also lose weight and stay satiated for a long time.

Coconuts are full of various antioxidants. Most of these antioxidants are phenolic compounds such as caffeic acid, gallic acid, salicylic acid, p-coumaric acid, etc. All these acids are good for the health of your body as they tackle free radicals.

It also contains a high number of polyphenols, which reduces the oxidation of LDL. Oxidized LDL leads to the formation of plaque in arteries.

Coconuts are extremely versatile, and they can be eaten in a variety of ways. Shaved or flaked coconuts are great for savory dishes. Shaved coconut is a great addition to rice, stews, soups, curries, etc. Certain brands of shaved coconut contain sugar, so it is best to avoid them if you want to lose weight.

Shredded coconut is great for desserts and baked goods. Raw coconut can add a really brilliant tropical flavor to any dish. If you are allergic to gluten, then you can replace wheat flour with coconut flour. This flower is also suitable for Paleo diet followers.

Coconut oil can be used for cooking, frying, baking, and roasting as well.

Garlic

Garlic has been used for its taste enhancing and medicinal properties since ancient times. Hippocrates, the father of modern medicine, used to prescribe garlic for a variety of ailments. Now modern science has confirmed and proved its health benefits.

Garlic is a member of the onion or Allium family. The members of this family, such as onions, shallots, etc. contain a lot of sulfur compounds that are responsible for the health benefits. One such compound is allicin. Along with allicin, other compounds that make garlic healthy include diallyl disulfide and s-allyl cysteine. Garlic is great for weight loss as it contains a very low number of calories. One clove of raw garlic has:

- 2% of daily manganese

- 2% of daily vitamin B6

- 1% of daily vitamin C

- 1% of daily selenium

- 0.06 grams of fiber

It also contains moderate amounts of copper, calcium, potassium, iron, phosphorus, and vitamin B1.

It contains only 4.5 calories and 1 gram of carbs. It also contains around 0.2 grams of protein. Garlic is good for the health of your immune system. It is effective against the common cold as well. It is also used to treat cough and sore throat.

Garlic is supposed to be great for the health of your heart as well. It is good for hypertension and high blood pressure, as well. Garlic can also reduce the levels of cholesterol and thus reduce the risk of heart diseases. It is really effective against LDL cholesterol.

Garlic is rich in antioxidants. These antioxidants can tackle free radicals and prevent oxidative damage as well. These antioxidants can also improve your immune system. According to some sources, garlic can also target Alzheimer's and dementia as well.

Garlic can also increase your longevity. It can tackle many different infections, as well as chronic diseases. Garlic also has detoxifying effects that can prevent organ damage by getting rid of harmful chemicals from the body. Another thing that makes garlic really great for health is that it can make your bones strong. It reduces bone damage, especially in the case of women. It can reduce the occurrence of osteoporosis in women.

Garlic is a versatile food item that can be incorporated into various recipes. It goes great with bread, soups, and sauces. Garlic has a strong taste, and thus, it can make otherwise bland food taste good. Garlic can be used in a variety of forms. The most commonly used forms are cloves. It is also possible to use garlic in the form of pastes and powders. Nowadays, garlic oil is used in a lot of cuisines as well.

Garlic can cause halitosis if used improperly. It is recommended to avoid using garlic if you are allergic to it. Garlic is also not recommended for people who are on blood-thinners.

Chapter 5 – 8 Reasons Why You Are Not Losing Body Fat

Collectively, we spend years of our lives trying to shed those extra pounds of body fat but have little to no success. We go on diet after diet, our weight yo-yoing up and down and we ride on a rollercoaster that has way too much roll in it. We try to shed the fat when we are motivated but still fall apart when we see a plate of fresh warm cookies. Unfortunately, this is why so many New Year's resolutions wind up discarded and gym memberships get ignored. While we might have a common goal in mind, losing fat, it is not an easy thing to achieve satisfactorily.

If you have been playing the same game and haven't yet succeeded, you are more than likely making a couple of mistakes. Below I am going to talk about the 8 most common mistakes that people make when they are trying to lose fat:

Mistake Number 1 – You are eating too much

This might seem like an obvious on but so many people seriously do not know how many calories they are eating. A salad might seem like a low calorie option but you may actually be munching your way through 600 calories. Salad dressings, sauces, ketchups and oils are all loaded with calories that you don't always see or think about, especially if you are not a regular cook at home.

We are always told to eat less calories than we are burning but this simplifies matters too much. This would work if you, for example, ate 1500 calories worth of cheesecake every day and burned 2000 calories. But, the one thing the human body can't do is be a calculator. What matters is not how many calories but the type of calories you are eating. If you eat a diet that is made up of carbohydrates only, you won't burn any fat, whereas if you eat less of the carbs and more protein, fat and the right carbs, you are on to a winning combination for burning fat and building up muscle.

Most people find that a ratio of 40% carbs, 40% protein and 20% fat works perfectly to burn off that fat. However, that may not work for all so you will need to do your research and work out what is best for you. Some people have to reduce their carb limit even lower to be successful but, if you have to do that, boost up your good fat intake to allow your body an alternative source of energy to burn.

Mistake Number 2 – You are not eating enough protein

Protein isn't just for building and repairing your muscle tissue. Recent studies have showed that, on two groups of women who were overweight, both of whom consumed the same number of calories per day, the group that consumed 128 g protein every day lost more weight than the group who consumed just 68 g protein per day.

Protein makes you feel fuller for much longer and stops you from grazing throughout the day and from eating too much at your main meals. A high protein diet can also affect the glucose levels, blood lipids and muscle to fat ratio in the body in a positive manner. Protein is an excellent fat loss macro but you will not see instant results by adding protein shakes to your diet. Fat burning is not instant; it takes dedication and consistently following the meal plan to make a difference. What you can do is add high protein foods to your meals and cut down on the bad carbs foods – you will see the results in time.

Mistake Number 3 – You are drinking too much

You really only need to drink water. You can have tea or coffees, occasionally milk but stop the stream of sugar-filled drinks. All they are doing is undoing the good work the rest of your food is doing. One pumpkin spice latte can contain over 300 calories, and that is just in one drink! That is not doing your body any good at all – all you are doing is making your fat loss goas harder to attain.

Alcohol is also a bad call. While a beer or a glass of wine every now and again isn't going to make much difference, you must stop the binging at weekends. Alcohol is high in calories, these are stored by your body as fat, and it also causes an impairment to your judgment. Instead of eating a good healthy choice, the booze will tell you that a big pate of cheesy chips is just the right thing to eat.

Mistake Number 4 – You think that healthy foods have no calories

Everything has calories in it, regardless of how healthy it is. If you eat too much, you will struggle to shed the fat. Of course, you need to eat whole foods but eating too much organic peanut butter is still overeating whichever you look at it. Two examples of healthy foods that are significantly high in calories are seeds and nuts. They contain micronutrients, omega 3 and phytogens that are absolutely wonderful for your health but are excessively high in calories. Don't avoid them; just stick to eating a small handful at a time.

Mistake Number 5 – Your training regime is not intensive enough

While it is important for complete beginners to start off slowly, you should gradually up your game, as you become more and more used to the gym machines, weights and the actual exercise itself. Start to push yourself harder and harder – if you get comfortable doing your training, your weight loss will simply plateau. If you are not breaking a sweat through your exercise, you are not working out hard enough. If you are not sweating, you are not burning fat and your heart rate is not working to your benefit.

If you are looking to burn fat, you need to create an extreme energy demand so that your body is able to change. Lifting the same old weights time and time again will not help you to burn fat and you won't be gaining any real benefits from your physical activity.

Mistake Number 6 – You are doing too much low intensity cardio training

Ok, so I just told you to up the intensity of your workout and now I'm telling you off for doing too much of something that isn't intensive. Cardio is not a form of resistance training. It is a completely different type of fitness and a two-hour slog on the treadmill is not going to give you the results that an hour of heavy lifting will.

If you want your cardio to work, do full body workouts that include a short rest period. By using your whole body and taking shorter breaks, your cardiovascular system and your muscular system are being challenged.

Mistake Number 7 – You are stressed out

Stress is one of the biggest and most silent killers. Stress causes your body to produce cortisol in levels way beyond what is normal. This can be responsible to an increase in fat storage in the body and many other negative consequences. Even if your diet and your training regime are spot-on, if you re stressed, you will not achieve your goals.

The key is to relax and, although that is easier said than done, if you can learn some deep breathing, meditation, or yoga and incorporate it every day in your diet, you will see a significant change in your overall health and in your physique

Mistake 8 – You are not sleeping enough

Sleek deprivation also raises cortisol levels and, when you are lacking in sleep; your insulin sensitivity is also reduced. Together, these two problems are not good news for anyone who wants to burn fat. Sleep is a priority in your life. You cannot possibly party all night and expect to function well the next day. Aim for 8 hours of good sleep every single night. Don't drink alcohol, don't use your tablet, mobile phone or watch TV for at least an hour before you go to bed, eliminate caffeine in the evenings and give yourself time to relax in the evenings.

Nicholas Bjorn

Chapter 6 – Eat Right For Weight Loss

From what most of you have read in numerous articles and papers and, of course, the grand old Internet, there are about a gazillion diets to follow. People religiously begin one in the month of January and drop out mid-way due to sheer fatigue, exhaustion, and the primal urge to eat. Almost all diets work in the short term - by eliminating one or more crucial food groups, such as carbs or fat or vegetables or any combination of the groups. That is why, by forcing yourself to eat fewer calories per meal, you definitely lose weight in the beginning. But later on, as your body demands the lost nutrition, you begin bingeing on unhealthy foods and snacks and promptly gain all the weight you managed to lose. That's sad, really. But there's no denying it - you can't fool your body.

But there's a way out. You really don't have to starve or deprive yourself of eating your favorite foods. You can do that and STILL beat the escalating calories. Is it magic? Is it like entering the world of wizards? Is it some alternate realm of reality?

Not really. It's a basic, most fundamental fact of biology. Losing weight happens simply because you consume fewer calories than you burn. That's it. No complicated charts and figures. If you eat less and expend more calories, you lose weight. How this happens is important.

First, we need to understand what a calorie is and what all the fuss is about it.

Simply put, a calorie is a unit of energy. All our foods and drinks give us some kind of energy, the fuel for our body. Carbohydrates, fats, proteins, minerals, and vitamins - all have calories. How much energy they give out is measured by calories. Each day, our body requires a certain number of calories for its normal function - for your heartbeats, brain activity, body functions, etc. So, just in order to EXIST, you expend calories. This is called the Total Daily Energy Expenditure or TDEE. For example, if you are a 40-year-old female, weighing 140 pounds and standing 5"5' tall, you burn 1350 calories by just existing. Similarly, the calorie expenditure of a 30-year-old male, weighing 240 pounds and being 6 feet tall is around 2300. Get a general idea?

Basal Metabolic Rate (BMR)

BMR is basically the number of calories required by your body for its daily function. This base number of calories is required for involuntary functions of the body, such as breathing, pumping of the heart, digestion, etc. According to the Academy of Nutrition and Dietetics, your BMR should not drop below 1200. If it does, it starts affecting your metabolism in a bad way. Muscle mass begins to decrease; body fat falls below acceptable levels, circulation and pulse rate is affected, brain function is affected. Your overall health declines, which is precisely what you DO NOT want.

Factors such as gender, weight, and height affect this number. For a rough estimate, about two-thirds of the calories you eat go into the daily function of your body. The other third portion goes into the motion-related activities of your body. This also depends on the activity levels of your body.

Sedentary Lifestyle: BMR x 1.2

Slightly Active: BMR x 1.375

Moderately Active: BMR x 1.55

Very Active: BMR x 1.725

Now, let us show you an example. You are a 35-year-old male, weighing 200 pounds and standing 72 inches tall (six feet).

Let's use some numbers:

Suppose you're male, 35 years old, weigh 200 pounds and are six feet even (72 inches).

BMR= 1882 calories

If you are a sedentary person, this number jumps to 2258. That means you need that many calories just to sustain yourself on a daily basis, do your tasks, work, etc. If you are a moderately active person, your TDEE comes to 2917.

Now see the difference between being sedentary and moderately active. It amounts to 659 calories. That equals one whole meal! And that is why I wrote in the beginning- we tend to underestimate how much we are eating, but overestimate how much we are expending.

When you eat something, your body has three categories to decide where all those calories will go:

- for fuel-burning

- for rebuilding muscles

- for storing as fat

When you expend as many calories as you consume, you reach something called a "calorie equilibrium." No more, no less. Just a pleasant state of homeostasis. If you want to lose weight, you will need to eat fewer calories. This forces your body to hit the calorie reserve it has to burn fuel.

Now, when you eat more and burn fewer calories, the body does not need the extra calories it just ate. So, they are stored as fat, a.k.a, weight gain. And when you begin to see sense and burn off those extra calories or eat a calorie deficit, you lose weight. Simple?

Sure, in theory. But life isn't this simple, right. We are super amazing at underplaying the amount of food we eat and overestimating the rate at which we burn it off. Human nature, really! The so-called cheat days between exercise regimes, the accidental over-eating of your favorite dessert at a party, or someone's birthday - these are just some of the umpteen excuses we give ourselves when confronted with the reality.

Metabolism and Weight Loss

Your resting metabolism slows down when you lose weight. This is a simple concept. Because there is less of you to fuel and process, your metabolism doesn't have to work that hard to keep your bodily functions intact and functioning properly. When you lose weight, you also lose some water, lean tissue, and fat. If you weigh less, it will have less weight to carry around; the heart will have to pump less, etc. The body will, therefore, burn fewer calories than it did when you carried all that extra weight.

If you look at estimates from a calorie calculator, here's how much the resting calorie burn is for three different weights.

- 2600 calories for 300 lbs

- 2300 calories for 250 lbs

- 2000 calories for 200 lbs.

See the difference? By weighing just 50 pounds less, you strike off 300 calories from your metabolism. But here's where things get interesting. There is something called "adaptive thermogenesis." It basically means that the body keeps adjusting itself to the number of calories consumed and burnt per day, and the process it takes to preserve the body fat within.

Our body is constantly wondering if it will get the next meal or not. Because it does that, it has a tendency to store the calories as surplus - just in case the Earth is invaded, and we are left without supplies. That is why even though people seem to lose a few pounds, they have to make a consistent and lifelong effort to keep the extra kilos off. Many other factors - such as environmental changes, psychological elements, medication, depression, emotional pain, anxiety, and other issues can trigger or change eating patterns.

Now, instead of worrying about calories every single time you look at food, it's far, far better to eat the healthy and right kind of foods in the first place. For example - protein (meat, legumes), carbohydrates (brown or white rice, quinoa, wheat), fruit and vegetables, nuts, dairy (if you are not lactose intolerant). Just keep eating these foods and stay happy, full, and healthy for a long, long time. These wholesome foods keep us full for a much longer time, yet aren't that calorie-dense. If you do this over a consistent period of time, you will lose weight.

So, what can you eat to lose weight in a healthy manner?

Protein

As you have learned already, protein is the building block for our skin, hair, and muscles. If eaten properly, it makes for a very filling and delicious food group. Generally speaking, you should eat about 1 gram of protein per lb. of bodyweight. Guzzling a can of energy drink will fill you up for about ten minutes. And leave you with loads of unwanted calories. The same amount of calories can be obtained from a good serving of chicken. Healthier, right? Because protein requires energy to metabolize, a high protein diet can be key for a calorie deficit. It fights the primary cause of weight gain - cravings. Protein can be found in meat, legumes, fowl, eggs, fish, etc. But try to keep the upper limit at 250 grams, because too much of anything can also cause problems.

Vegetables

No, pizza is not a vegetable. Real vegetables are rich in nutrients and calorie-light. That means you can eat a lot of these and feel full but are very unlikely to gain weight. Every meal should have at least two servings of differently colored vegetables - the more color, the better. Seasonal vegetables work best. Broccoli, spinach, cauliflower, radish, Brussels sprouts, kale, zucchini, cucumber, carrots, onions, potatoes, asparagus, etc. are some veggies to get you interested!

Fat

Yes, I said fat. Fat has always been vilified, but healthy fats work wonders for your body and especially for your skin. Foods such as avocado, nuts, olive oil, peanut butter, whole milk, grass-fed butter, etc. contain healthy fat needed by the body. Consume these in small amounts to reap maximum benefits and also lose weight in the process.

The Grain is a Go-Go

Instead of highly processed junk food like pizza, burgers, patties, ready to eat meals and soups, cakes and cookies, go for whole grains. Choose whole-wheat pasta, brown bread, bran, rye crackers, etc. These will fill you up and keep you satiated for a longer time.

Minimize Processed Food

If it's not growing on a tree or swimming in the sea or pulled up from the Earth, don't bother eating it. Processed food is designed to be super tasty but, in reality, contains a whole lot of preservatives and additives. It does make people addicted to it.

Oversee Liquid Calories

Fruit juices and those who say "enriched fruit or energy water" are nothing but sugar in a liquid form. All of your sodas and colas also fall into this category. Liquid calories account for why people can't seem to lose weight even after switching to healthier diets. Even seemingly harmless coffee orders contain lots of cream and sugar. These drinks and beverages have no fiber and only sugar inside them, which wreaks havoc with our bodily systems. Alcohol also does the same - provide empty calories and a hangover which nobody wants. Sugar not only causes obesity but a host of other diseases. If you want your weight loss to work, drink lots of water, black or green tea, or sparkling water. That's it, no sugary beverages.

Drink More Water

This is such an important point; it has been dealt with in another chapter in the book. Drinking water has been found to increase the number of calories you burn. Studies have shown that drinking about eight glasses of water per day is equal to having burnt about 96 extra calories. Sweet deal! Of course, WHEN you drink, it is also important. Drinking water half an hour before meals help reduce hunger, and thus, you eat less, creating a calorie deficit. Also, drinking water half an hour after meals are also beneficial to digestion.

Because the thirst and hunger centers are located so close to each other in the hypothalamus, most of the time, in between meals, we tend to feel hungry when, in fact, we are THIRSTY. Drinking water will curb this pang of false hunger, and you will eat properly when the actual mealtime comes around.

Condiments and Accompaniments

If your healthy broccoli, pear and carrot salad has a generous overdose of ketchup and mayo over it, or if you dunk everything in heavy sauces and dips, the actual nutritional value becomes less. Keep an eye on what you put on your veggies and meats.

Smaller Meals

Food nutrition experts also recommend that you eat smaller meals and pace them throughout the day. This keeps your blood sugar levels in check and also stops you from overindulging on unhealthy snacks.

Smart Substitutions

Don't want to eat salad by itself? Add some vinegar, soy sauce, and basil for an instant livening up of the situation. Homemade salsa and hummus, mustard paste, homemade white butter for your jacket potatoes, basil and cilantro, lemon, and vinegar are all healthy complements and dressings for your pasta, salad, and toppings.

What Else Can I Do?

Predetermine your Meals

I know it sounds like a boring and tedious activity. But picture this - you're home tired after a long day's work, and maybe managed to squeeze in some exercise in between. But you're too tired to cook, so you just order some pizza and a soda, and all your hard work go down the drain. Pre-plan and pre-cook your meals and bung them in the freezer. It makes a world of difference in your weight loss journey.

Strength Train

I can't stress this enough. When you lift weights, you force your muscles to break down. And when you rest and eat properly, the muscles rebuild themselves and take the fuel from the stores available in your body. That means, even as you are resting, you are burning calories. It's a win-win all the way - as you keep getting stronger, your muscles become bigger, and you keep losing body fat. This is also an important aspect of losing weight and maintaining it and is discussed in a separate chapter.

Calorie Deficit

Consistently maintain a calorie deficit. You can also mix and match your exercise routines to include cardio, strength training, Zumba, Pilates, yoga, etc. and continue with your healthy weight loss journey.

Step Up!

Even if you can't find the time to strength train, you can always start walking. That remains the best and most natural exercise ever designed for the body. Move constantly. Park your car a few hundred yards from your office or home. Take the stairs at work. Walk back from the supermarket. Run around with your dog or your neighbor's dog. March in place while watching advertisements. Just keep moving it.

Close your Kitchen at Night

Late-night snacking in front of the TV, eating because you don't have anything else to do or simply dipping your hand inside the cookie jar every time you enter the kitchen - these are just some of the ways in which you pile on unnecessary pounds. Set a time for your meals and stick to it. Get into the habit of closing up the kitchen after a set time, say 9 p.m. No going into the kitchen or fridge after that. If it helps, brush your teeth an hour after eating. The minty taste will let you forget any mindless snacking you might want to indulge in.

Controlling your Immediate Environment

If your fridge is always stocked with pastries, cakes, sodas, pizzas, and the like, it's very unlikely that you will reach for a bag of cauliflower or carrots when there is an appetizing cheese burst pizza staring at you. Make it a point to stock your pantry and fridge with healthy foods - vegetables, fruit, healthy cuts of meat, nuts, olive oil, whole grains, popcorn, lemon water, etc. so that when you feel the urge to snack or make yourself a meal, you reach out for real food.

One Step at a Time

I get it. You're ambitious and want to lose ten pounds by this Saturday. But if you cut back on your favorite foods, begin a vigorous strength training regime, say bye-bye to alcohol and keep moving all the time - you will most definitely hit a plateau very soon. Take it slowly. Cut back on one unhealthy snack per week. Or have one glass of wine in two weeks. Go for a walk first instead of lifting weights straight away. Take it slowly and steadily.

Check Food Labels

Whenever buying something from the market, be sure to check the nutrition label on the back. If it lists more than ten chemicals and just one or two real food names, chuck it back on the shelf. It's not worth eating it. For example - potato chips should be just that; Potatoes, oil, and salt rather than some twenty triglycerides and ten preservatives shown on the label.

Forgive Yourself

If you ate unhealthy food at one meal, it's okay. It's not the end of the world. Get back on track with your next meal.

You can use some popular apps to keep track of how many calories you are consuming. My Fitness Pal, Fat Secret, and Lose It are three of the most popular ones right now.

Of course, you can't be tracking your food for the rest of your life. But, when you're starting out, it helps to know how much you are eating. That will help you see if you are going overboard with some food groups or ignoring something else completely. Portion sizes also matter here. Let's show you an example.

One pound of fat is equal to something like 3500 calories. So, if you wish to lose one pound of fat per week, you need to eat 500 calories less per day. You can do that either by cutting out 500 calories or burning them through exercise. And arguably, it is much more difficult to increase time for activity levels than it is to reduce calorie consumption. Let's face it - if given a choice, which would you pick? Incorporating thirty minutes or more of exercise time in your schedule or giving up and substituting a food group in your diet?

You guessed it.

Let's take 200 calories as a measure. 200 calories of broccoli would fill up a dinner plate. The same 200 calories are found in half a Snickers bar. How many people you know would prefer eating broccoli to a bar of chocolate? And is it easier to eat a full plate of broccoli than a tempting half bar of yummy chocolate? And who the heck ever eats HALF a bar of chocolate?

That is why you need to eat REAL foods.

Nicholas Bjorn

Chapter 7 – Planning Your Meals

Meal planning may seem to be quite a difficult task, but it really isn't. It is easy and doable if you know and understands what you are doing. In simple terms, meal planning means planning your meals for the week and keeping things ready for these meals. This way, you can save a lot of time and money. Meal planning can be divided into three sections:

- Select the recipes

- Shop for the ingredients

- Prepare the ingredients

Many people find meal planning difficult because many myths that are prevalent about it. For instance, a lot of people believe that you need to plan meals by noting them down in huge binders, which you need to lug around all the time. But this is false; you can make simple meals in Google Docs or any notepad application on your phone. If you do not like using your phone for lists, you can also make simple lists on paper and post it on your fridge.

Many people also think that meal planning is only suitable for large families. But this is false. You can make meal plans for yourself as well. This is especially recommended if you are trying to lose weight or are an extremely busy person. It is also recommended for people who are trying to save money.

Meal planning does not take a lot of work, especially if you have the basics ready. Once you have the basics ready, you can make meal plans for every week in less than an hour.

Meal plans are extremely flexible, and you can change and experiment according to your needs and desires. Nothing is set in stone in the world of meal plans.

Beginning a Meal Plan

Before making a plan, you need to ask yourself:

Why do I need a meal plan?

There are no wrong answers to the above question, but focusing on the reason will allow you to concentrate effectively. In the beginning, keep your reasons and meal plans simple. You can increase the difficulty level with time and experience.

Once you have understood your reason behind meal planning, you can now start with the plan itself. As said above, the first step for meal planning is choosing recipes.

Choosing Recipes

Choosing recipes is a simple task if you know the reason behind your meal plan. For instance, if you are making meal plans because you want to lose weight, it is recommended to choose only healthy recipes. Similarly, if you are making meal plans because you are trying to cut down your expenses, then you should choose recipes that do not require a lot of exotic or expensive ingredients. Thus, you need to focus on the reason behind your meal plan all the time. Never choose recipes randomly. Similarly, avoid making meal plans a day before (at least in the beginning.) Give yourself at least three days to make a meal plan and prepare for it.

If you eat out frequently, add these outings to your meal plan. Once you decide the days and meals, you can move on to the recipes. It is recommended to choose recipes according to your schedule. For instance, if you are generally the busiest on Thursdays, you can either opt for a simple recipe, or you can opt for a recipe that can be made in a slow cooker. This way, you can just add the ingredients to the cooker in the morning and let it cook over low temperature until you return. If you work late on Mondays, you can make more food on Sunday and carry it the next day.

Once you have noted down the recipes, it is now time to get the ingredients.

Ingredients

To make the shopping easy, it is recommended to make two-ingredient lists- a master list and a grocery list. Two lists may sound to be a lot more work than one single list, but making a master list will help you a lot in the long term. The master list will help you keep a stock of fresh and dried ingredients in your pantry, and you won't have to buy them every week.

Master List

In this, add the ingredients that are used in almost all the recipes. You can also add ingredients that are generally purchased in bulk on this list. Try to avoid easily perishable ingredients to this list.

Grocery List

In this list, add anything that can be stored for at least a couple of days. This should include vegetables, dairy, eggs, etc.

Once you have collected the ingredients, the next step in meal planning is preparing them.

Keeping your ingredients prepared is a great way to save time and money. Keeping things prepared is especially great for people who want to avoid working on weekends. Keeping things prepared can help you avoid frustration and fatigue. It will allow you to have more free time for yourself. It is recommended to set aside a few hours on Sunday (or any other day that you are free) and prepare your ingredients according to your meal plan. For instance, if you plan to make salads on Monday or Tuesday, it is recommended to chop some things and refrigerate them. Similarly, if you plan to make pasta or any similar product, you can keep the ingredients for the sauce, such as garlic, etc. ready. Keeping things clean can also save you a lot of time.

Meal plans are simple and effective if you know how to craft them and follow them successfully.

Chapter 8 – The Importance of Water

Water, water everywhere; all the boards did shrink,

Water, water everywhere, nor any drop to drink

The Rime of the Ancient Mariner

Water is everywhere around us, isn't it? That gorgeous pool, those tantalizing lakes and ponds, those mighty seas and majestic oceans of the planet. Over 80 percent of the planet is basically water. And it's the same case with our bodies too. Water makes up a whopping 65 to 70 percent of our bodies. Two atoms of hydrogen, one of oxygen. And it powers the planet. It's not only vital for life to survive and thrive. Going without it for as little as three days will send you into an irreversible spiral of decline.

Now, why is this compound so essential to our health?

Water performs some of the most important functions of the human body: flushing out waste products, regulating body temperature, keeping homeostasis going on properly, aiding brain functions, and more.

Benefits of Drinking Water

Creation of Saliva

Do you know how dry and irritable the mouth gets when you have a fever or some other disease that dries up your mouth? You miss your saliva terribly during those times. Saliva is nothing but water, mucus, and enzymes that break down your food and keep your mouth healthy and germ-free. If you drink water regularly, your body produces enough saliva for proper function. A dry mouth usually indicates dehydration.

Regulation of Body Temperature

Every time you breathe or blink, you lose water through the pores of your skin and eyes. Hydration of the body is vital for the proper regulation of your body temperature. You lose more water through sweat when you exercise or live in hot environments. Sweating keeps your body cool, but the temperature will rise if the loss of water is not replenished. So, keep drinking water to keep your basal metabolic temperature right.

Protection of Tissues, Joints, and Spinal Cord

Water acts as a lubricant and cushions your bones and joints from everyday jarring and bumping around. It eases their function.

Waste Removal

Water is like a carrier of waste material outside your body. By way of sweating, urination, and defecation, water helps flush out toxic waste from your body. Not doing so will result in painful constipation, kidney problems, kidney stones, metabolic breakdown, and a slow build-up of toxins in the body. A build-up of waste in the body can result in bloating and gas in the stomach. People may also feel very lethargic. Generous doses of water throughout the day can help curb this problem.

Maximize Physical Activities and Exertions

During physical activity, a lot of water is lost due to perspiration. Athletes may lose up to 6 to 10 percent of body weight during rigorous training. Drinking plenty of water during such activities helps keep the body cool and energized. Not being hydrated affects your strength and stamina for sports and physical activity. If you exercise in the heat, without drinking adequate water, you may be in danger of serious medical maladies such as heat stroke, hyperthermia, low blood pressure, etc.

Prevention of Constipation

Fiber is a must to have smooth and easy bowel movements. But water aids immensely in the process too. If you don't drink water throughout the day, you might have constipation. The only way out is to drink a couple of glasses of water, wait for an hour or so and then go to the restroom. You will find that the bowel movement is now significantly easier.

Aids in Digestion

Drinking water half an hour before and after meals has been proven to have a positive effect on weight loss and digestion. When you have it before eating, you feel less hungry and eat less. When you drink water half an hour after meals, it won't interfere with the natural digestive processes and helps churn the food easily.

Nutrient Absorption

Water also helps your body to absorb nutrients, vitamins, minerals from food, and delivers these important components to the rest of the body for its building and strengthening activities.

Weight Loss

There are numerous studies linking weight loss and water consumption. While dieting or exercising or just eating healthy, drinking water in adequate amounts also amounts to losing extra pounds.

Fights off Illnesses

Drinking enough water is a natural remedy to ward off diseases like kidney stones, urinary tract infections, hypertension, etc. Water is also a carrier of essential nutrients and vitamins throughout the body, so whatever you eat will be distributed well.

Boosts Energy

Metabolism is also affected by water or lack of it. Drinking water activates the metabolic levels, which, in turn, boosts the energy levels. Studies have shown that as little as 500 ml. of water can increase the metabolism by about 30 percent.

Mood Enhancer

I'm sure you've had bad days, or know of people who became grumpy for no reason at all. Dehydration is also a cause of these kinds of mood swings. It results in fatigue, anxiety, and grumpiness. A bit of water will do the trick!

Skin Lover

We all know the benefits of water for our skin. As the water flushes out toxins from the body, the water which goes into our cells plumps them up. This, in turn, plumps up the skin cells and surfaces and also promotes collagen production, resulting in fewer wrinkles and a more youthful you!

Prevention of Overall Dehydration

We all know how dangerous dehydration is. Severe dehydration can result in kidney failure, brain swelling, seizure, and other body dysfunction. Water helps prevent all these situations. Keep drinking enough water at intervals to sustain a healthy body.

How Much Water Should I Drink?

According to the National Academies of Sciences, Engineering, and Medicine, these are the guidelines for water intake for most people:

Around 125 ounces each day for men and 93 ounces for women. Of course, it all varies depending on the type of work one does and the environment one lives in. Food gives us about 20 percent of our daily intake of water. Everything else depends on how much water and how many water-based drinks you ingest throughout the day.

The color of your urine and thirst you experience are also indicators of your hydration levels. Pale yellow-colored urine is a good indication, while dark yellow means you need to drink more water.

Keep a bottle of water with you and drink from it at regular intervals. As a rule of thumb, aim to drink at least three to four liters of water in a day. Of course, if you end up drinking too much water, that will cause irreparable damage to your body and brain. Just drink enough to sustain and maintain good metabolism.

Water and its Many Forms

Water is just that, right? Plain old boring water? But what about juices, sodas, smoothies, colas, sugary teas, etc.? Sure, they are hydrating and feel particularly great on a hot day, but they also contain enormous quantities of sugar and unwanted calories. Coffee and tea are diuretics - they make you lose water. Alcohol also gives the impression of being hydrating, but it actually has the opposite effect. The same goes for sports drinks. Though they contain electrolytes and other energy-giving substances, they also contain sugar and salt, which is more than the recommended amount. Pay attention to the number of such drinks when you do consume them.

The Role of Water in Weight Loss

Many studies have highlighted the correlation between drinking water and weight loss. Let us see how it does that:

Burns More Calories

When you drink more water, it increases the number of calories burnt by the body, also known as the "resting energy expenditure" of the body. Some studies have shown that within 10 minutes of drinking water, the energy expenditure increases by about 30 percent! And this effect lasts for a whole hour. Another study conducted among overweight women showed that drinking just one liter of water extra per day resulted in a loss of almost 2 kilos over a period of a year. There were no other control variables here - no exercise or lifestyle changes. Just the additional drinking of one liter of water. Therefore, the results are really impressive. Also, the study revealed that just half an extra liter of water per day would cause you to burn 23 calories. This results in a massive 17,000 calorie burn over the whole year!

Natural Appetite Suppressant

We have spoken about the hunger and thirst centers located in the hypothalamus, in a different section of this book. When the stomach senses that its capacity is now full, it sends a signal to the hypothalamus, which in turn gives a feeling of "fullness" to the eater. Drinking water before meals can fool the brain into thinking that it is somewhat full, thus avoiding overeating. Because those two centers are so closely located, a person may think he or she is hungry, when thirst might be the actual issue. Drinking water also curbs unnecessary snacking between healthy meals.

Curbs Unwanted Liquid Calorie Intake

Sodas, colas, sugary drinks, fruit juices, etc. contain a large amount of sugar, which needlessly build-up problems in the body. Drinking water at regular intervals ensures that one doesn't fall prey to such liquid calories.

A Friend to Fat Burning

Water is essential to help burn fat. Without adequate water in the body, the process of metabolizing fat, called "lipolysis," cannot occur properly. The first step, called "hydrolysis," happens only in the presence of water - where the water molecules interact with triglycerides for the creation of glycerol and fatty acids. You have to drink enough water to keep this process going on smoothly and to burn fat effectively.

Workout Helper

Eating healthy and exercises are two sides of the same coin. And water helps immensely with exercise and workouts. It lubricates the joints, muscles, and tendons effectively and makes them more pliable for exercise, thus helping you on your way toward a healthy and happy body.

Nicholas Bjorn

Chapter 9 – Strength Training: A Vital Component of Your Weight Loss Journey

When you exercise and pick something you love to do, you give the best workout to your body and mind. You are also motivated further to keep eating healthy and keep moving.

Don't feel like exercising? It must be something you LOVE to do. Don't do it because your neighbor/friend/dad told you to. If you hate running or gymming or Pilates, don't do it! Pick something you love and stick to it.

Remember, you read somewhere in this book that whatever you eat is taken inside by the body for three functions: fuel, storing as fat, and rebuilding muscles, when you weight train and challenge your muscles beyond their capacity, the body's sorting behavior changes.

There's really nothing like lightweight training, so we'll leave that. A heavy workout would include a 500 lb. deadlift or 450 lb. squats. Intense bodyweight training for strength might include a handstand push up or 100 pull-ups in a minute. You get the drift.

Now when you weight train - you pick something heavy and move it against gravity for a certain number of times - your muscles break down. When you rest, eat, and sleep, they rebuild themselves in the next 48 hours. So, talking about the redirecting of calories, which happens, the body sends those calories to rebuild the broken down muscles. Also, it will direct the additional calories to burn as fuel to handle all this intense lifting activity.

So what does that mean for metabolism and weight loss? Metabolism gets a boost, and you burn calories even as you are sitting. Now, when you eat a calorie deficit and then strength train, your body gets even cleverer and stronger over time, resulting in serious weight loss without any loss in muscle mass.

Now, here's a scenario for you: You are weight training, your muscles are breaking down and need rebuilding. Because you are eating less than usual, there aren't enough calories ingested as compared to the number needed for the rebuilding process. So, what happens? Is it not worth doing all of this?

Of course not!

This is where our amazing body comes into play. Remember the "Reserve Store of Fats"? Yep. The body pulls out calories from this reserve stock and happily goes about rebuilding the muscles. You just need to keep eating enough and eat foods based on your exercise and diet goals.

Resting properly is also an important part of rebuilding muscle and keeping them strong for the next workout. This, in turn, will promote hunger at the right time, and you will eat only the right foods for your body.

Chapter 10 – Kitchen Implements and Gadgets for Healthy Cooking

Now that you are truly on your way to eating and living healthy, why not arm yourself with the right kind of tools and gadgets which will help you stick to your health plan? Here's a handy list of implements to have in your kitchen.

Steamer

Steam your vegetables for salads and veggie bowls easily.

Handheld Spiralizer

No more buying noodles and pasta from the take-out! Just use this handy spiralizer to carve your own noodles and pasta shapes at home.

Blender

A godsend for kitchens. Blend your fruit and nuts into smoothies, whip up healthy juices, and just about any dip or sauce that you like. All at the press of a button!

Nonstick Grill

This can be electric or the one you set on the stove. Grill your meats and sandwiches to perfection with the nonstick grill. Some even come with a charcoal flavor, to give you that barbeque feeling.

Rice Cooker

Another life-saving device. You can bung in your rice, measure out the water, and turn it on. By the time you're done with other activities, your rice is also done. Simply take it out and have it with whatever meats or veggies you cooked.

Nonstick Frying Pan

Takes up less oil, and you also get your meats and veggies out of it cleanly and easily.

Handheld Immersion Blender

This is different from the regular blender. With this, you plunge the blender into the foods you wish to blend. Making buttermilk, squashes, and other quick mixing drinks has never been easier!

Vegetable Peeler cum Julienne

This gadget allows you to do two things. Julienne, or cut vegetables into thin, long sticks and also peel tough veggies such as carrots and gourds.

Measuring Cups

Of course, at some point, you will want to bake and cook like a pro. These measuring cups come in very handy, having all kinds of metric conversions and quantities written clearly.

Tupperware and Prep Containers

After having worked all that hard to cook, you may have leftovers. Keep them fresh and safe inside Tupperware containers, which are microwave and dishwasher safe.

Food Processor

If you can afford this, congratulations. You've saved yourself precious hours in the kitchen. A food processor will do all these for you - chopping, dicing, slicing, shredding, mincing, pureeing, and even mixing batters and doughs! A small kitchen miracle in itself.

Nicholas Bjorn

Chapter 11 – Refrigerator Essentials for Healthy Eating

When you are surrounded by packets of chips, cans of soda, bags of pretzels, or boxes of pizza, it's really hard to even begin thinking healthily. Why not stock up your larder and refrigerator with something healthy, so that whenever you feel hungry and reach out, you will always hit something which is real food - not junk food.

Here are some foods and condiments you can keep in your fridge/pantry/freezer for continuing your healthy streak:

1. Basic Vegetables: You can store veggies like carrots, beans, celery, bell peppers, eggplant, etc. because they can stay for at least a week or so in the fridge. Just put them inside mesh bags so they can breathe properly.

2. Fruit: Apples, pears, grapes, melons, berries, citrus fruits can be stored for a good amount of time in the fridge. These make for a very healthy and tasty snack too.

3. Greens: The thing with greens is that they begin to wilt and spoil easily. So, keep your greens like kale, spinach, cilantro, and lettuce in large mesh bags or containers with drainboards underneath them. Keep them this way for a week at most.

4. Herbs: The top choices for herbs are cilantro, thyme, parsley, sage, rosemary, and dill. These can be stored fresh or in the dried form. If fresh, wrap them in dry paper and store.

5. Dried fruit: Another quick snack is dried fruit and nuts. You can store almonds, cashews, peanuts, cranberries, blueberries, dried figs, apricots, and raisins for a really long time. Use them in baking and cooking and enjoy the delicious taste. A small handful of nuts is enough to fill you up for a long time.

6. Milk: Keep a variety of milk such as almond, cashew, soy, rice, or hemp milk easily available at markets. Use them in breakfast cereal, baking, or cooking. But yes, have them sparingly.

7. Eggs: One of nature's best and cheapest nutritional hacks. When you're hungry, just boil a couple of eggs and have them with some salt and pepper. Or, scramble some eggs with butter and seasonings and have it on top of whole-wheat toast. The possibilities with eggs are limitless and equally healthy.

8. Salsa: You can either make your own salsa or buy a jar from the market. It is a delicious dip, dressing, and sauce - or simply have it with some baked sweet potato fries.

9. Mustard: Another delicious fall back option for sandwiches, stir-fries, sauces, and dressings.

10. Yeast: Store this in the active or dry form. Yeast adds a cheesy flavor to foods and is used in baking - for bread and pizza bases. Try some in your pasta and savory dishes as well.

11. Miso paste: This is a mild yet rich flavoring agent. Try it with your sauces and dips.

12. Tahini/ Nut butter: A super delicious and healthy snack would be nut butter with some crackers. Peanut and

almond butter are especially suitable for this purpose, and can also be used with sandwiches and baked stuff.

13. Soy sauce: Mostly used in Chinese cooking along with vinegar and chili sauces, you can also use soy sauce as a dressing or in salads or just one spoonful of it in a sauce - to embrace its taste and goodness.

14. Cacao powder: A fat-free and super yummy baking essential, keep some handy in your pantry or fridge to quickly whip up delicious low-calorie desserts.

For Your Freezer

1. Cooked beans: Suppose you made an extra helping of beans. Save time for the next meal by simply freezing this portion. To reuse, thaw the bag out in the fridge overnight, or run hot water over them and consume.

2. Cooked grains: Because grains take a long time to cook, it makes sense to make a larger quantity and freeze the leftovers. Storing cooked grains like rice and quinoa in the freezer will make the next meal planning a breeze.

3. Frozen vegetables: Frozen veggies such as corn, peas, carrots, cauliflower, edamame, etc. will ensure that you always have a healthy meal option to fall back on, instead of relying on take-outs.

4. Frozen fruit: Whenever there is a grocery sale, stock up on basic fruit like berries, apples, bananas, lemons, cantaloupes, grapefruit, etc. Again, a time-saving meal option.

5. Ginger and garlic: These are basic seasoning herbs and freeze very well too. Just grind together equal quantities of ginger and garlic, fry them in a little oil and when cool, put in freezer bags and freeze. Whenever you want to make a meat or veggie-based dish, just put together your frozen veggies, take the herbs from the fridge and cook them with some pre-roasted ginger and garlic and you have a meal ready in no time!

6. Corn, Rice, and Wheat Tortillas: You can quickly make wraps, tacos, and quesadillas if you have a ready store of these items in your freezer.

Chapter 12 – How to Eat Healthy Without Going Broke and Losing Your Mind

Now, eating healthy and all is great. But if you're a college student or someone who is on a tight budget or similar, it's more tempting to give in to a cheap bagel or pizza at the diner than laboriously check grocery prices and lug home bags of produce and herbs. It is even easier to just pop in a bag full of Doritos rather than get up earlier in the mornings to pack your lunch.

Yep, I hear you. But, it turns out, there are easy hacks everywhere. You can begin your healthiness quotient right now.

Love coffee and can't give it up? Cut back just one cup a day. Or bring in some homemade coffee in a flask. Another better option is to switch to green tea. Leave your tea leaves at work and bring along a hot water brewer. There is really no downside to deciding to start eating healthy. The thing is- when your body keeps getting empty calories by way of unhealthy snacks, it assumes that it will go on forever. When you suddenly start feeding it healthy stuff, it will rebel for a few days, then quickly adjust. The cravings slowly disappear, and the body starts demanding and utilizing healthy food you put into it. All this will result in a happy and sound you!

Shopping the Right Way for Health

Frequent One or Two Stores

Of course, keep an eye out on different offers, but frequent one or two places where you've been before. Check what is on sale and pick the best foods in that. Meats, veggies, fruit- doesn't matter. Pick out the best and freshest produce on display, not necessarily based on the menu you have planned for the week. Bring everything home, and THEN plan your menus. It will save you a lot of time and money.

Get Creative while Cooking

Let's say a recipe calls for green peppers, but you have yellow ones. Or it says hummus, and you forgot to buy chickpeas. There are always substitutions available. Check your pantry and fridge. Use yellow bell peppers instead of green. Or, use some miso dip instead of hummus.

Prepare Meals in Advance

It's quite easy to do this. You can chop your veggies and make batters or doughs while binge-watching your favorite shows. Even better, you can cook your chicken and veggies, portion them out and freeze them in individual serving boxes. That way, you just have to bung one in the oven before you come to work and won't have to depend on any store-bought food item for your lunch.

Buy in Bulk

Whenever possible, look out for bargains in meats and produce. Buy a whole bunch of it when on sale or discount, chop them into meal-sized portions and either freeze them immediately or cook them and then freeze.

Eat Small and Healthy Snacks

Stuff like fruit, peanut butter on crackers, carrot sticks, sprouts, popcorn, nuts are all healthy and filling snack options if you get hungry in between meals.

Eat Everything You Buy

More often than not, we go out in a rush and buy tons of food and produce and stash it all in the fridge. After about a week of hard work cooking and making meals, we fall off the wagon, and all that food keeps rotting inside the fridge. That's such a waste of money. Make it a point to stock only about a week's worth of produce and meats in your fridge and EAT ALL OF IT before you buy new food.

Learn to Cook

It doesn't necessarily have to be a Michelin rated meal. Even something as simple as scrambled eggs on toast, chicken breasts marinated and grilled, healthy low-fat sandwiches or rice wraps filled with vegetables are all great and simple starting points for meals. Pick one simple recipe and master it. Then another, and another. You can definitely learn to cook elaborate and complicated meals later on, but for now, this will do.

Chapter 13 – 15 Tasty Super Food Smoothies Recipes

The following recipes all contain superfoods and are another alternative as a way of making sure that you get all you need in your diet. With the smoothies, simply add all the ingredients to your blender, whiz them up and enjoy!

Peanut Butter Power Shake

- 1 scoop of whey protein powder, chocolate flavored
- 1 tbsp. organic or natural peanut butter
- ½ banana
- 1 cup of almond milk
- Ice cubes

Dark Chocolate Shake

- 1 scoop whey protein , chocolate flavored
- 1 cup almond milk
- 2 ½ tbsp. cacao powder
- 2 ice cubes

CHIA Green Smoothie

- 1 scoop whey protein vanilla
- 1 tbsp. chia seeds
- 1 cup spinach
- 1 cup almond milk
- 1 banana
- water/ice

The Winter Mint Chocolate Shake

- 1 scoop whey protein , chocolate or chocolate mint
- 1 cup almond milk
- 1/2 cup arctic zero mint chocolate
- 1 drop peppermint extract
- 2 ice cubes

Green Spinach-Apple-Mango Yogurt Smoothie

- 3/4 cup plain 0% Greek yogurt
- 1/2 bunch spinach
- 1 apple
- 1/2 cup mango chunks
- 1 cup ice/water

Anti-Aging Kiwi-Blueberry Smoothie

- 1/2 scoop whey protein , vanilla
- 1/2 cup 0% plain Greek yogurt
- 1 cup flax milk
- 2 kiwi
- 1/2 cup blueberries
- 2 ice cubes

Berry Banana Smoothie

- 1 scoop whey protein , vanilla
- 1 cup flax milk
- 1/2 cup blackberries
- 1/2 banana
- 1/2 cup raspberries
- 1/2 cup strawberries
- 2 ice cubes

Peach-Mango Yogurt Smoothie

- 1 Cup plain 0% Greek yogurt
- 1 peach
- 1 cup mango chunks
- 1/4 tsp. cinnamon
- 1 cup ice

The Lean Muscle Mochaccino

- 1 scoop whey protein, mocha cappuccino
- 1.5 cups flax milk
- 2.5 tbsp. cacao powder
- 2 ice cubes

Orange Creamsicle Smoothie

- 1 scoop whey protein, orange creamsicle
- 1 medium orange
- 1 cup almond milk
- 1/2 cup orange juice
- 1 cup water/ice

Liquid Breakfast Smoothie

- 3/4 cup plain 0% Greek yogurt
- 1/2 banana
- 1/4 cup rolled oats
- 1 cup strawberries
- 1 cup water/Ice

Banana Nut Shake

- 1 scoop vanilla whey protein
- 1 cup almond milk
- 1 large banana
- 3 tbsp. organic peanut butter
- water/ice

Strawberry Shortcake Smoothie

- 3/4 cup plain 0% Greek yogurt
- 1 cup strawberries
- 1/2 cup rolled oats
- 1 tsp vanilla extract
- water/ice

Mango Pineapple Shake

- 1 scoop vanilla whey protein

- 1/2 cup mango chunks

- 1/2 cup pineapple chunks

- 1 cup almond Milk

Creamy Chocolate Avocado Smoothie

- 1 scoop chocolate whey protein

- 1/2 small avocado

- 3/4 banana

- 1 1/2 cup ice/Water

Chapter 14 – 5 Tasty Super Food Soup Recipes

Green Superfood Soup

Ingredients:

- 185 g broccoli
- 2 leeks sliced
- 1 onion roughly diced
- ½ teaspoon garlic oil or minced garlic
- 1 cup green split peas – soaked for 1 hour, rinsed
- 310 g medium cauliflower
- 9-10 g dry wakame seaweed – soaked for 10 min, roughly chopped
- 80 g kale – roughly chopped
- ½ cup stock
- pinch sea salt
- pepper
- ¼ tsp thyme
- enough water to cover
- Oil for cooking

- Coconut cream

Instructions:

1. Heat up the oil in a large pan

2. Cook the onions and leeks until they are brown

3. Add all other ingredients, add the stock and enough water to cover the vegetables

4. Simmer for about 1 hour over a low heat, or until the split peas are soft

5. Blend in the blender to make a thick soup

6. Add in some coconut cream and water to bring it to the consistency you like

7. Season with salt and pepper

Carrot and Turmeric Soup

Ingredients:

- 500 g carrots
- 2 garlic cloves
- 1 onion, white
- 1 tbsp. coconut oil
- 2 tsp turmeric
- 1 tbsp. fresh ginger
- 400 ml stock
- 150 ml water
- Salt and pepper
- 1 lime

Instructions:

1. Chop the carrots into pieces about an inch in size and peel the garlic; set aside

2. Cut the onion into small bits and fry over a medium heat with a pinch of salt and 1 tbsp. oil

3. Add the ginger and turmeric and cook for 30 seconds, stirring

4. Crush the garlic and add it in, stir and add the carrots

5. Roast for a few minutes before adding the stock

6. Use a blender to blend the soup until smooth – add more water if needed

7. Add another inch of salt, pepper and squeeze the juice in from the lime

Dairy-Free Creamy Avocado Soup

Ingredients:

- 3 ripe avocado, peeled, pitted and chopped
- 2 cups plain dairy-free yogurt
- ⅓ cup cashews
- ⅓ cup finely chopped fresh cilantro
- ⅓ cup Vidalia onion, chopped
- 1 Tbsp. white balsamic vinegar
- 1 cup green tea, brewed and chilled
- 1 tsp. sea salt
- ¼ tsp. freshly ground white pepper
- 2 chives, finely chopped

Instructions:

1. Blend the avocado, yoghurt, cilantro, almonds, onion, vinegar, green tea, pepper and sea salt until smooth
2. Transfer into a bowl and cover; refrigerate for 2 hours
3. Serve chilled and garnished with chopped chives

Nicholas Bjorn

Spicy Chicken and Quinoa Soup

Ingredients:

- 2 tbsp. extra virgin olive oil
- 1 cup diced onion
- 2 garlic cloves, chopped
- 2 tomatoes, peeled and diced
- 2 carrots, peeled and chopped
- 1 tsp of paprika
- 2 tsp of cumin
- 2 cups of white meat from 2 baked skinless and shredded organic chicken breasts
- 2 cups of filtered water
- 4 cups low sodium organic chicken broth
- 2 cups of fresh or frozen peas
- 2 cups cooked quinoa
- 4 tbsp. finely chopped parsley
- 3 tbsp. finely chopped cilantro
- 1 tsp kosher salt
- Freshly ground black pepper

Instructions:

1. Heat up the olive oil in a large soup pot

2. Add the onions, garlic and sauté until translucent, about 5 minutes

3. Add the tomato, carrots, cumin and pepper, cook for a father 5 minutes, stirring

4. Add the water and broth, turn the heat up to high and bring to a boil

5. Add the peas, quinoa, herbs and chicken, season with salt and peeper

6. Reduce heat and simmer for 25 minutes

7. Serve hot with a diced avocado

To Bake Chicken Breasts

1. Preheat the oven to 350° F

2. Rub olive oil over the chicken and season with salt and pepper

3. Place in a foil lined baking sheet, skin side up and bake for 40 to 45 minutes

4. Remove and allow it to cool off before taking the skin off and shredding it

Slow Cooker Superfood Soup

Ingredients:

- 2 cups sliced carrots
- 1 large sweet potato, cut into 1/2" cubes
- 1 cup fresh or frozen green beans
- 1/2 cup fresh cilantro, chopped
- 1 small onion, diced
- 1 clove garlic, minced
- 2 (15 ounce) cans black beans, drained and rinsed
- 1/2 teaspoon crushed red pepper flakes
- 1/2 teaspoon black pepper
- 1 teaspoon chili powder
- 1 teaspoon cumin
- Kosher or sea salt to taste
- 2 cups vegetable juice (I used R.W. Knudsen, Organic Very Veggie Juice, no sugar added)
- 2 cups vegetable broth, low-sodium

Instructions:

1. Mix all the ingredients together in your slow cooker, cover and cook it for about 6-8 hours on low, or until the

vegetables have gone tender. If you want, you can add in a tbsp. of low fat cheddar cheese

You can sauté onion in 1 tbsp. olive oil for 5 minutes and then add the garlic and sauté for a further 1 minute before adding them to the slow cooker. You can also add in 2 cups of coarsely chopped kale about 5 minutes before the end of cooking

Nicholas Bjorn

Chapter 15 – 6 Yummy and Healthy One-Bowl Meals

Quinoa and Chicken Burrito Bowl with Green Sauce

Ingredients:

For the quinoa:

- 1.5 cups pre-washed quinoa

- ¾ tsp salt

For the chicken:

- 2 pounds chicken tenderloin or boneless chicken pounded to ½ inch thickness

- 5 tbsp. extra virgin olive oil

- 2 tsp honey

- 4 garlic cloves, minced

- ½ tsp ground black pepper

- 1 tbsp. lime zest (from two limes)

- 1-1/4 tsp chili powder

- ½ tsp coriander (fresh or dry)

- ¼ tsp dried oregano

- Salt: As per taste

For the green sauce:

- 1 jalapeno chili pepper, seeded and chopped

- 1 cup cilantro leaves

- 2 garlic cloves, chopped

- ¼ cup sour cream

- ½ cup mayonnaise

- 1 tbsp. fresh lime juice

- 2 tbsp. extra virgin olive oil

- Salt and pepper - As per taste

Instructions:

The Chicken

1. Mix all the ingredients except the chicken breasts in a large freezer bag. Close it and thoroughly mix all the ingredients together.

2. Add the chicken breasts into the marinade and mix until every piece is evenly coated with it. Seal the bag and put it inside the fridge (preferably in a bowl) and let it marinate for at least 6 hours or overnight.

3. When it is fully marinated, take the bag out of the fridge.

4. Clean your grill and put it onto preheat. Spray it with a nonstick cooking spray or lightly coat the grill with oil until it is well oiled.

5. Take the chicken pieces out and lay them on the grill. Slowly grill them for two or three minutes on each side and transfer to a plate. Cut them into bite-sized pieces.

The Quinoa

1. Mix the quinoa, salt, and around two and a half cups of water in a saucepan.

2. Let it come to a boil, then reduce the flame and cover.

3. Cook for ten to fifteen minutes until the quinoa absorbs water and gets cooked. When done, take it out in a bowl and keep aside.

The Sauce

1. Mix all the sauce ingredients in a blender and combine to make a smooth puree. Taste and check for seasonings. If you wish to make it in advance, you can put this sauce into a bowl and refrigerate it until you want to eat.

How to Assemble

Get your quinoa bowl in front of you. Put the grilled chicken on top, and pour the sauce over it. If you wish, you can add additional toppings like tomatoes, diced pumpkin, carrots, or celery.

French Lentil Salad with Goat Cheese

Ingredients:

- 1 cup French lentils (or any other lentils)
- 3 ounces goat cheese
- 3 cups chicken broth
- 1 large carrot, finely chopped
- 2 celery stalks, finely chopped
- 1 small bay leaf
- 1 tsp fresh thyme
- 3 tbsp. parsley, chopped
- 2 garlic cloves, chopped
- 1 tsp mustard
- 1 tsp honey
- Salt: As per taste

Instructions:

1. Wash and rinse the lentils well.

2. Mix lentils, chicken broth, and bay leaf in a saucepan. Let it boil for a few minutes, then simmer them over low heat

until the lentils are soft and tender. This may take about 20 to 25 minutes.

3. After this, remove the bay leaf and drain the water from the lentils.

4. In a bowl, mix together all ingredients except the goat cheese.

5. When the lentils are cool, add them to the bowl, adjust seasonings and toss to combine well.

6. Just before eating, crumble the goat cheese over the salad and serve. You may wish to serve the salad with fresh iceberg lettuce leaves.

Thai Chicken Soup with Rice Noodles

Ingredients:

- 4 cups chicken broth
- ½ cup shallots, thinly sliced
- 2 tbsp. Thai green curry paste
- 1 tbsp. vegetable oil
- 1 tbsp. fresh ginger, minced
- 2 tbsp. fish sauce
- 1 can coconut milk
- 4 heaped tsp brown sugar
- 2 tbsp. fresh lime juice
- ½ tsp turmeric
- 1 pack rice noodles

Instructions:

1. Heat the oil in a medium-sized saucepan or soup pot.

2. Add the ginger and shallots and cook for a few minutes, stirring constantly. Don't let the ginger burn.

3. Mix in the curry paste and cook for a minute.

4. Add the chicken broth, coconut milk, brown sugar, fish sauce, turmeric, and lime juice. Add salt if you wish to.

5. Bring to a simmer and gently cook for about five to six minutes.

6. While this is happening, make the rice noodles according to the instructions on the package.

How to Assemble

Adjust seasonings in the soup. Pour the soup over the rice noodles and gently give it a mix. You can serve this with cilantro or celery, and chopped scallions. You may also drizzle some Sriracha sauce over it.

Cauliflower Fried Rice

Ingredients:

- 2 lb. cauliflower

- 4 to 5 tbsp. vegetable oil

- 2 large eggs, beaten

- 2 scallions, chopped finely

- 3 garlic cloves, chopped

- 1 tbsp. freshly chopped ginger

- 4 tbsp. soy sauce

- 1 cup peas and carrots (frozen peas and carrots also work)

- ¼ tsp red pepper flakes

- 1 tsp honey

- 1 tsp rice vinegar

- 1 tsp sesame oil

- ¼ cup chopped cashews/ almonds/ peanuts

- Salt: As per taste

Instructions:

1. Grate the cauliflower, either by hand or in a food processor.

2. Heat the vegetable oil in a large skillet or cast iron pan.

3. Add the eggs and salt and keep cooking until the eggs are scrambled and cooked. Keep aside on a small plate. Carefully wipe the pan.

4. Again, add about 3 tbsp. of vegetable oil to the pan and keep it at medium heat. Add in the scallions, garlic, and ginger and cook gently.

5. Mix in the grated cauliflower, red pepper, soy sauce, honey, and salt. Keep stirring.

6. Then add the peas and carrots and keep cooking until the cauliflower is soft and the vegetables are tender.

7. After five minutes, add the rice vinegar, sesame oil, and nuts.

8. After about two minutes, add the eggs. Keep tasting and adjusting the seasoning.

9. Take off the fire and serve right away with a dash of soy sauce on top.

Thai Shrimp and Quinoa

Ingredients:

- 1 pound raw jumbo shrimp (cleaned, deveined and tail off)

- 2 cups chicken stock

- 1 and a 1/2 cups quinoa, uncooked

- 1 cup coconut milk

- 1 tbsp. coconut or any other oil

- 1 tbsp. fish sauce

- ½ cup small onion, chopped

- ½ tsp sesame oil

- 1 each, red and yellow bell peppers, chopped

- 2 medium carrots, julienned

- ½ tsp ground ginger

- Salt: As per taste

- 3 cloves minced garlic

- ¼ tsp red pepper flakes

- ½ a lime, chopped

Instructions:

1. Take a large cast-iron pan or skillet and heat the oil for a couple of minutes.

2. Add the fish sauce and sesame oil and stir.

3. After a couple of minutes, add the bell pepper, carrots, and onion and ginger. Add some salt at this stage.

4. Cook for four or five minutes until the vegetables become tender.

5. Now add the garlic and cook for another minute.

6. Add the coconut milk, quinoa, and chicken stock. Mix well, cover, and cook for almost 15 minutes until the quinoa is fully cooked.

7. Once done, remove the lid and add the shrimp to the mixture.

8. Adjust seasoning and add pepper flakes to it. Cover and cook for five to six minutes until the shrimp is translucent and cooked.

9. Serve hot with wedges of lime and a dash of cilantro on top.

Ratatouille Rice

Ingredients:

- 1 tbsp. olive oil

- 1 medium onion, diced

- 3 cloves minced garlic

- 1 medium zucchini, diced

- ½ eggplant, diced

- 1/8 tsp ground black pepper

- ½ tsp dried oregano

- ¼ tsp red pepper flakes

- 1 red bell pepper, diced

- 2 small tomatoes, diced

- 1 cup white rice

- 1 cup vegetable broth

Instructions:

1. Take a skillet and warm the olive oil for a minute.

2. Add in the onion with a bit of salt, and cook until it becomes translucent and tender.

3. Add the garlic and cook until it gives off a nice aroma.

4. Now add the eggplant, zucchini, black pepper, oregano, pepper flakes, some salt, and stir. Cook this for about a minute or so.

5. Then mix in the tomatoes and bell pepper and cook until the tomato starts releasing oil and liquid around it.

6. Lastly, add the white rice and vegetable broth. Stir until combined and bring to a boil.

7. After a couple of minutes, simmer the mixture and cover and cook for about 18 minutes, until the rice is completely cooked. If you feel the rice is sticking to the bottom, add some more broth.

8. Check seasonings and add pepper, salt, herbs as desired. Serve this healthy dish hot from the stove, garnished with cilantro and basil.

Chapter 16 – Sweet Endings: Lip Smacking Healthy Desserts

So you thought desserts are the work of the Devil, full of rich and sinful things that you eat just once and repent at leisure? Do not fret. Here are some absolutely delicious desserts for you to indulge in, without going off the health wagon.

Avocado Chocolate Mousse with Summer Fruit

Ingredients:

- 4 ripe avocado

- ¼ cup coconut milk

- 4 tbsp. dark cocoa powder

- 3 tbsp. honey

- 2 ounces dark chocolate, melted (70 percent or more cocoa)

- 2 tsp vanilla extract

- 1/8 tsp salt

- Coconut whipped cream, strawberries, blueberries, and other summer fruit, chopped

Instructions:

1. Peel and pit the avocado and put them inside a food processor.

2. Blend until well combined and creamy.

3. Mix in the cocoa, honey, milk, vanilla, chocolate, and salt. Keep blending until they mix properly. Taste at this point and add more honey if desired. The mixture should be completely creamy at the end of this.

4. Serving: Take out into pretty bowls and top with coconut cream or layer it with summer fruit such as berries, mangoes, even nuts and add a few nuts for extra crunch.

Raspberry Vegan Cheesecake

Ingredients:

For walnut crust

- 1 cup walnuts

- 3 dates (Mejdool or similar), pitted

- ½ tbsp. coconut oil

- ¼ tsp sea salt

For the raspberry layer

- 12 ounces frozen raspberries

- ½ tsp fresh lemon juice

- 2 tbsp. maple syrup

- 2 tbsp. chia seeds

Instructions:

1. Blend together the walnuts, salt, dates, and coconut oil in a food processor until the mixture turns crumbly.

2. Line an 8" by 4" loaf pan with parchment paper. You can also butter it beforehand. Press the crust onto the bottom and freeze until the next layer is ready.

3. Blend together the thawed raspberries, maple syrup, lemon juice, and chia seeds. The mixture should be smooth; no bits should be visible. Pour this mixture over the frozen walnut crust and smooth it out. Freeze this for at least four hours.

4. When you are ready to serve this dessert, take the cake out of the freezer and let it thaw for about twenty minutes.

5. Lift it out carefully from the pan. Slice into as many slices as you would like. Garnish with a sprig of mint for extra flavor.

Cinnamon Baked Pears

Ingredients:

- 2 pears, washed, cored and cut in half

- 1 tsp cinnamon

- 1 tsp maple syrup

- Pumpkin spice granola and coconut cream for toppings

Instructions:

1. Before doing anything, preheat the oven to 350 degrees.

2. Take a baking sheet and place the pears on it. It should stand straight on the paper. Or you may cut into any shape you desire or even bite-sized pieces.

3. Sprinkle it evenly with the maple syrup and cinnamon. Bake this for about 25 minutes.

4. Cool them and top with either the granola or any other nuts or berries and enjoy.

Healthy Peanut Butter Fudge

Ingredients:

- 2 cups finely shredded coconut

- 1 cup creamy peanut butter

- ½ cup coconut oil

- 4 tbsp maple syrup

- 1 pinch sea salt

- 1 tsp vanilla extract

- Toppings: peanuts, coconut flakes, nuts, etc.

Instructions:

1. First, line a 9" by 5" loaf tin with parchment paper.

2. Add the desiccated coconut to a food processor and blend on high speed until the mixture becomes creamy. Scrape down the sides and keep aside.

3. Add the peanut butter and coconut oil and blend one again at high speed.

4. Once done, mix in the maple syrup one tablespoon at a time. Check for sweetness and add until the desired level is reached. Don't add too much because then the coconut mixture with seize and you won't be able to work with it.

5. Add sea salt and vanilla extract and mix well.

6. Transfer this to the loaf pan or tin and spread it evenly all over. At this point, you can also add some crunch on top by putting nuts or flakes.

7. Now freeze this until it becomes firm. Take a knife and run it through hot water and cut the mixture into even squares. This will give you about twenty squares.

8. Serve immediately and enjoy it. You can also store these in the freezer for up to a month.

No-Bake Brownie Energy Bites

Ingredients:

- ½ cup each walnuts and almonds

- 1 cup dates, chopped

- 1/3 cup plus 2 tbsp. unsweetened cocoa powder

- ½ cup shredded coconut flakes

Instructions:

1. Grind together the walnuts and almonds in a food processor. The mixture should form a dough.

2. Mix in the dates, coconut, cocoa, and a pinch of salt and incorporate it well into the dough.

3. Now, lightly grease your palms with coconut oil or use saran wrap to make balls out of the dough.

4. Roll these into the remaining coconut flakes or use corn flakes or almonds to coat the balls. Put them inside the fridge for a little while. Take them out and serve.

Apple Crumble

Ingredients:

- 5 apples, Granny Smith or similar
- ½ cup low-fat butter
- 3 and a half tbsp. flour
- ½ cup honey or maple syrup
- 1 lime
- 1 small stick cinnamon
- 1 tbsp. sugar
- Coconut cream: Optional

Instructions:

1. Preheat the oven to 180 degrees Celsius.
2. For the topping, take the butter in a plate and sift flour over it.
3. Add the honey. Mix these by hand until you get a crumbly mixture.
4. Peel the apples and cut them in half or bite-sized pieces. Place these in an ovenproof bowl.

5. Squeeze the lime over them and shake so that it is distributed equally, and the apples are not discolored. Sprinkle the one tablespoon sugar over them. Put in the stick of cinnamon over this.

6. When ready to go inside the oven, sprinkle the topping you just made over the apples. Bake for about 40 minutes, till the apple crumble turns golden brown.

7. Serve either hot or cold with coconut cream.

Yogurt Cocktail

Ingredients:

- 1 and a half cups yogurt or curd

- ½ cup plums

- 4 medium strawberries

- ¼ cup pineapple

- 4 tbsp. honey

- ½ tsp vanilla extract

- ½ cup non-dairy cream or coconut cream

- A few cornflakes- different flavorings

Instructions:

1. Chop the fruit into bite-sized pieces and put the mix in a big microwaveable bowl. Add some honey and microwave them on high for a minute.

2. Combine the yogurt, remaining honey, and vanilla in a bowl.

3. Add the coconut cream and mix well. Either put it in the fridge or strain through a muslin cloth to get rid of excess water and then put it in the fridge, depending on how you like the consistency.

4. Take the fruit bowl out of the microwave.

5. Layer the fruit one by one alternating with the yogurt mixture in a large glass bowl. For garnishing, use cornflakes or coconut flakes or any nuts of your choice.

Quick Coffee Dessert

Ingredients:

- 2 eggs

- ½ cup ground sugar or maple syrup

- A pinch of salt

- 1 tbsp. instant coffee

- 1 cup whipping cream or nondairy cream

- 2 tbsp. castor sugar

- 1 tsp vanilla extract

- ¼ tsp almond essence

Instructions:

1. Put the eggs, salt, and sugar in a bowl and beat with a hand mixer at high speed. The mixture will become lemony and fluffy.

2. Add the coffee and beat for a few more minutes. Keep this aside.

3. In another bowl, take the cream and sugar and whip until soft peaks form. It shouldn't be too runny or too stiff. Gently stir in the essences.

4. Fold the egg mixture into the cream and combine gently, making sure you don't lose the aeration.

5. Pour into individual glasses and freeze until you are ready to eat.

6. When serving, take the glasses out and let them sit for about ten minutes or so before digging in. If you wish, garnish with mint leaves.

Simple Rice Pudding

Ingredients:

- ½ cup rice washed and soaked in ½ cup low-fat milk

- 5 and a half cups low fat milk

- ½ cup sugar or honey

- Almonds: Blanched and slivered, a few

- Rosewater: A few drops

- Pistachios: A few

Instructions:

1. Blend the rice and milk, such that it becomes an absolutely smooth paste.

2. Take the other milk in a vessel and boil it. Pour the rice-milk paste and sugar or honey into it and continuously stir it on a low flame until the mixture thickens. Simmer for a while.

3. Take it off the fire.

4. Add the almonds and pistachios, along with the rose water and mix well. Pour into glasses or bowls and chill well. Serve with a glass of cold milk, if so desired.

Rich Chocolate Slices

Ingredients:

- ½ cup butter or low-fat margarine
- 2 tbsp. honey
- 4 and a half tbsp. cocoa
- 225 grams semi-sweet biscuits
- 2 tbsp. raisins
- 2 tbsp. chopped mixed nuts

Instructions:

1. Mix the honey, cocoa, and butter in a pan and put it on a gentle heat. You will need to keep a watch over it and remove it as soon as the butter melts.

2. Mix the ingredients of the pan well and keep aside.

3. Meanwhile, crush the biscuits in a clean bag with a rolling pin or blend in a processor. You can do the same with the nuts. Keep aside.

4. When the butter mixture cools down, add the biscuit and nut mixture to it. Mix well. The final consistency should be crumbly, yet it should hold well when you compress it.

5. Grease a small cake tin with oil or butter and pour this mixture into it. Leave it inside the fridge to set.

6. For serving, let it rest on the countertop or dip the tin into hot water for a few seconds and invert it over a plate. Cut into slices and serve with fresh fruit on the side.

Nicholas Bjorn

Conclusion

If it wasn't clear from the beginning, stop chasing the latest diet trend and focus on the healthy weight loss and super foods in this book. Know that you can eat normally and still lose weight.

Your next step is to follow the strategies and recipes listed in this book. Apply what you have just learned. Take action and be consistent! The best thing you can do to lose weight and be healthier is to eat right.

Now, I would love to hear what you think! Please let me know if you enjoyed this book or what I could improve on. You can do that by leaving a review on Amazon. I'll be looking for your reviews when I come back to add more content my book. Thank you in advance!

Thank you, and good luck!

Nicholas Bjorn

Nicholas Bjorn

FREE E-BOOKS SENT WEEKLY

Join <u>North Star Readers Book Club</u>
And Get Exclusive Access To The Latest Kindle Books in
Health, Fitness, Weight Loss and Much More…

TO GET YOU STARTED HERE IS YOUR FREE E-BOOK:

Visit to Sign Up Today!
<u>www.northstarreaders.com/weight-loss-kick-start</u>

Nicholas Bjorn

References

https://www.healthline.com/nutrition/top-10-evidence-based-health-benefits-of-coconut-oil#section10

https://www.ausnaturalcare.com.au/health/life-style/lifestyle/food/goji-berries-real-superfood

https://www.healthline.com/nutrition/11-proven-health-benefits-of-garlic

www.webmd.com

www.self.com

www.mayoclinic.com

www.nerdfitness.com

www.buzzfeed.com

www.tasty.co

www.healthline.com

www.jamieoliver.com

Nicholas Bjorn

GOOD NUTRITION IS IMPORTANT – THIS IS A FACT.

BUT HOW DO YOU REALLY GET STARTED TO ACHIEVING IT? PEOPLE SAY IT BEGINS WITH A BALANCED DIET, BUT HOW EXACTLY DO YOU ACHIEVE THAT BALANCE?

If you are lost in the world of calories and kilojoules, this book is the perfect reference to help you! The contents of this book will help you focus on what's important while getting rid of all the unnecessary fluff about dieting and healthy living that are just bound to confuse you.

Here is what this book has in store for you:
- Nutrition defined and simplified
- Dietary guidelines made easy to follow
- Nutrition labels made understandable
- Vitamins and minerals explained
- Fat-burning foods enumerated
- Meal planning and recipes made doable

Start reaping the benefits of eating healthy and living healthy! You can get started today.

Visit to Order Your Copy Today!
https://www.amazon.com/dp/1519485492

DO YOU WANT TO KNOW HOW YOU CAN LOSE WEIGHT AND BUILD MUSCLE FAST, STARTING RIGHT NOW? THIS BOOK WILL LET YOU IN ON THE SECRET!

Everyone knows how important it is to maintain a healthy physique. Often, achieving the ideal body requires you to lose weight and build lean muscle. But how do you do that? To become physically fit, you need to have the knowledge necessary to get you on your way and the motivation required to keep you going.

Here's what this book has in store for you:
- Learn how your body uses calories and what role carbohydrates play in your weight
- Discover which foods contain good fats and lean protein that could benefit your body
- Determine what your meal frequency and caloric intake should be
- Know which exercises you should do to get that toned and sculpted look

With the knowledge you will gain from this book, you will be on your way to getting the amazing body that you want!

Visit to Order Your Copy Today!
https://www.amazon.com/dp/1514832968

Printed in Great Britain
by Amazon